Getting a PhD

SCHOOL OF ORIENTAL AND AFRICAN STU

Compared to their previous experiences, new PhD students face very different challenges and responsibilities, require different skills and must achieve higher standards of performance. Where do research students get such information?

This book provides guidance that will help research students avoid needless mistakes and address the demands of their PhD research project with confidence. It informs and advises research students on many of the important facets of postgraduate research, including:

- explaining what it means to conduct research at doctoral level;
- the doctoral requirements for independence, contribution to knowledge, originality and suitability for publication;
- getting the most from your supervisor;
- planning a research project;
- conducting a literature review;
- writing the thesis;
- publishing your research;
- criteria used in the PhD examination.

Each chapter contains reference to selected reading and online resources, and there are numerous exercises that encourage you to consider how the content applies to your research project.

Getting a PhD is an essential handbook for PhD students, and will provide plenty of valuable advice for Master's students or undergraduates conducting a research project.

John A. Finn is Research Officer at Teagasc, Ireland, where he manages research projects and supervises PhD students. He is also Visiting Researcher at University College Dublin.

Getting a PhD

An action plan to help manage
your research, your supervisor
and your project

John A. Finn

Routledge
Taylor & Francis Group

LONDON AND NEW YORK

First published 2005 by Routledge
2 Park Square, Milton Park, Abingdon, Oxon OX14 4RN

Simultaneously published in the USA and Canada
by Routledge
270 Madison Ave, New York, NY 10016

Routledge is an imprint of the Taylor & Francis Group

© 2005 John A. Finn

Typeset in Goudy by
Keystroke, Jacaranda Lodge, Wolverhampton
Printed and bound in Great Britain by
T J International Ltd, Padstow, Cornwall

British Library Cataloguing in Publication Data
A catalogue record for this book is available from the British Library

Library of Congress Cataloging in Publication Data

ISBN 0–415–34498–0 (pbk)
ISBN 0–415–34497–2 (hbk)

To my parents, for the educational opportunities
that they gave me, and to Linda, Gearóid and Aisling

Contents

List of illustrations

Figures

Tables

Acknowledgements

My decision to write this book was partly inspired by my interactions with Julian Park and Anne Crook during the following projects: 'Guidance for Students Projects' (GSP, http://bio.ltsn.ac.uk/hosted/GSP/) and 'Scientific Training by Assignment for Research Students' (STARS, http://www.ucc.ie/research/stars/). In addition to collaborating with Anne and Julian on the above projects, I am also very grateful for their enthusiastic discussion on many aspects of undergraduate and post-graduate research training, PhD supervision and for insightful feedback on this manuscript.

I am most fortunate to have benefited from the co-operation and assistance from a number of people. I am particularly grateful to Alan Kelly for his careful reading of several drafts of this book and support during the writing process. In addition to generously providing me with the benefit of his feedback and insights, he specifically suggested Figure 2.1 and initially discussed what evolved to be the description of adaptive management in Chapter 3. I have thoroughly enjoyed our discussions, which provided much-needed motivation on several occasions.

John Connolly and Paul Giller provided useful discussion and feedback, and I thank Joy Collier, Mark Fellowes, Con O'Rourke and Mary Smiddy for comments. The research staff and students at Teagasc provided valuable feedback, comments and support on many occasions, particularly Owen Carton, Donnacha Doody, Ed Dunne, Deirdre Fay, Liam Gaul, Kirsty Hooker, Fionn Horgan, Isabelle Kurz, Kay O'Connell, Norma O'Hea, Karl Richards, Rogier Schulte and Helen Sheridan.

I am grateful to Philip Mudd of Routledge and to many other colleagues who agreed that there was a need for a book such as this one.

For permissions and other assistance, I am grateful to the following: Vernon Trafford and Shosh Leshem kindly provided their list of questions in Chapter 7 and Tyrrell Burgess Associates provided permission to

reproduce this list from *Higher Education Review*; Michael Talbot gener-
ously agreed to the use of material from his lecture 'Aspects of scholarly
research: originality in scholarly writing'; Lynne Baldwin and Tomas
Roslin for permission to reproduce extracts from referee's reports written
by them (Chapter 6); the Dean of Postgraduate Studies, James Cook
University, Australia, for permission to refer to their *Handbook for
Research Higher Degree Students*; Ingrid Lunt at the Institute of Education,
University of London, for permission to reproduce their criteria for
examining the PhD (Chapter 7); Ellen Pearce of the UK GRAD Programme for permission to reproduce the Joint Skills Statement (Chapter
1), which was jointly developed by the UK Research Councils, Arts and
Humanities Research Board and UK GRAD programme, and David
Stannard and Richard Ellis of The University of Reading for providing
and permitting use of their Code of Practice on Research Students.

Finally, I would like to thank my family, Linda Moloney, Gearóid Finn
and Aisling Finn for their support and patience, without which I could
not have completed this work.

John Finn
July 2004

Introduction

The aim of this book

In many cases, the only difference between a new PhD student and a final year undergraduate student is a three-month summer break. Yet, compared to undergraduate students, PhD students face very different challenges and responsibilities, different skills requirements and higher standards of performance. No one is born knowing these things – so where do research students find such information?

Many institutions and supervisors provide excellent induction, support and training for research students; sadly, many do not. Even then, most training efforts tend to focus on research methods. Therefore, in many cases, it seems that students find their information (and misinformation) about strategically important issues in their doctoral project *via* what may be described as a form of social osmosis that derives from other research students, supervisors, research staff, and a variety of fragmented sources!

Experience is a valuable teacher, and an important view of the doctoral research project is that it is an opportunity to learn the craft of research, which relies strongly on learning by doing, and sometimes involves learning from mistakes. I agree with this view; some mistakes offer a very rewarding learning experience and are an important element of research training and practice. Nevertheless, other mistakes offer a minor learning experience and, too often, research students receive hard lessons from needless mistakes that could easily be avoided. For the sake of a lack of a little relevant information, these needless mistakes are repeated anew by successive cohorts of research students. In addition to being intensely frustrating, this is also a costly learning process in terms of finance, time and research quality.

This book aims to provide information that will help avoid some of these needless mistakes. It also aims to inform and advise research students on many of the important facets of postgraduate research. These include, for example: a clear understanding of what it means to conduct research at doctoral level; an awareness of the importance of conceptual development and critical evaluation; the ability to plan a research project over a substantial period of time (which requires strategic thinking and detailed planning); responsible research practice; the effective communication of your research in the written thesis and published papers, and the criteria used in the examination for the PhD degree. To this end, the book provides an overview of the terrain, and although there is no substitute for exploring it yourself, you should be guided away from dangers and pitfalls and toward more traversable ground.

This book is written primarily for research students pursuing a PhD degree; however, with minor alteration in interpretation, the vast majority of the content is also applicable to students pursuing a Master's degree and to undergraduate students conducting a final-year research project.

The PhD degree – variation in implementation

The 'typical' PhD student is registered for a full-time course of at least nine academic terms (three years) during which they pursue original research under the guidance of at least one research supervisor who is a member of staff at a university. The research is evaluated on the basis of a written thesis that is about 60,000 to 80,000 words long and an oral examination. This description, of course, ignores the huge variety of other circumstances that are found. For example, PhD students may be part-time and/or non-national; new PhD students may be progressing directly from an undergraduate degree or may be mature professionals with considerable experience; a supervisor may have little or a lot of experience in either student supervision or research; there may be an oral examination, there may not. Different countries, and different universities within a single country, also have different approaches to the PhD. As an example, many universities in the United States have a PhD programme that begins with a period (about two years) of taught courses and research training, which is followed by about two years of original research. Traditional PhD programmes in many other countries consist of a three-year programme of research that corresponds closely to the above 'typical' scenario. Even then, universities are increasingly adopting a preparatory year of taught classes, followed by a three-year PhD, the so-called '1+3' approach.

Thus, one of the difficulties in providing guidance for PhD students is the differences in local interpretation and application of regulations pertaining to the PhD degree. Throughout the book, therefore, I repeatedly advise that you consult with your supervisor (or otherwise find out) about the compatibility of the general advice in this book with the specific situation in your university.

The PhD degree – similarity in purpose

Given the considerable variation across institutional approaches to the PhD, it would be a worrying prospect if institutions had unique definitions and expectations from the PhD degree. Happily, this is not the case. The PhD degree, as defined by institutions and as experienced by research students, is generally underpinned by remarkably similar guiding principles and operational approaches. As a result, one can identify research experiences and issues that are widely shared by PhD students (e.g. see Table 3.2), which both justify and facilitate the formulation of general guidance. This book, therefore, is structured around important elements of the research process as experienced by doctoral research students; although the product of their research differs significantly across different research disciplines, the research process has many shared activities (see Chapter 1).

Outline of the book

Research students encounter different challenges as they progress through their research degree. The book is structured so that the earlier chapters are more relevant to postgraduate students who have just begun their research, whereas the later chapters are more appropriate to students who are nearing completion. Nevertheless, I would advise students at the beginning of their research degree to at least skim through the whole book so that you are aware of the content and can consult the appropriate sections in more detail as your research progresses.

Chapter 1 provides some indication of what to expect when doing a PhD, and focuses on the expected standard from doctoral research. An awareness of such issues is crucial if the doctoral thesis is to meet the required level of quality when it is examined. The chapter finishes with an overview of the educational benefits of a PhD degree, including a description of the range of skills that you will learn and implement during your doctoral project.

The relationship between students and their supervisor is a defining feature of the doctoral experience. Chapter 2 discusses the duties and responsibilities that supervisors should undertake; similarly, the duties and responsibilities of the PhD student are described. The chapter provides guidance on how to maximise the benefit of the finite amount of time that your supervisor can devote to your project. Some common problems associated with research supervision are discussed, along with some preventative and ameliorative strategies.

Project management is increasingly being recognised and adopted as a practical approach to help PhD students to manage their project. Chapter 3 introduces the principles of project management that are most relevant to PhD students, and focuses on different issues to be addressed when planning, scheduling and implementing your doctoral project. Specific examples are provided, and there is a consideration of the role of project management in facilitating the process of discovery that underpins original research.

Chapter 4 focuses on the aim of the literature review to provide a critical evaluation of a body of knowledge (an important requirement of the PhD thesis), and describes a number of strategies and examples. Chapter 5 discusses the process of writing and the importance of writing as a method that not just assists, but *is part of* your thinking, learning and understanding of your research subject. The written thesis must address the examiners' expectations of it, and this chapter suggests several strategies for doing so, along with relevant examples.

Chapter 6 gives an overview of the process that is typically involved when publishing your research in a journal. For example, it addresses the pros and cons of publishing during your PhD project, and discusses entitlement to authorship. The peer review process is described and there are examples of the issues that journal referees identify in their reports on submitted manuscripts.

Chapter 7 discusses the examination for the award of PhD degree, which is comprised of the examination of the thesis and the oral examination. Examples are provided of the criteria that are used in the examination of the PhD. The chapter concludes with a consideration of how PhD graduates may expect their skills to translate into professional practice in their future career.

Although this book aims to cover some of the common research processes that PhD students implement and issues that they encounter, it does not, and could not, cover all of them. A (very) much larger book would probably include a discussion of the principles of research design, statistical analyses, presentation of research findings (orally or by poster), financial issues, the added challenges of being registered part-time or studying abroad, the use of computer software, intellectual property rights, and so on. I certainly do not consider such issues to be unimportant. However, I believe that the treatment of strategic research processes dealt with in this book will enable you to deal with other such issues in two ways. First, through being more aware of your responsibility and ability to manage your research project and your professional development, you will more quickly recognise an 'issue' when it arises. For new PhD students, this is often a problem – they are simply so new to the postgraduate research culture that they are unable to recognise which issues affect them. Second, having identified an issue, you will be more aware of the various sources of help and assistance. Remember, *no one is born knowing these things*. Locate and read the information that can help you, and don't be afraid to ask your supervisors and fellow research students for guidance.

Throughout the book, relevant examples are used to illustrate various points. The subject matter of the examples is intended to reflect a variety of disciplines across the sciences, social sciences and humanities. The examples should be easily understood, and the research principles being illustrated should be applicable across many disciplines. There are also a number of Exercises that encourage you to engage with the issues on a more personal level, and provide an opportunity to reflect on how the content of a chapter or section applies to your specific research project. These exercises may be challenging or time-consuming to varying degrees, but they should provoke you to evaluate your understanding of what it means to undertake research that attains a doctoral standard. The relatively modest effort to conduct these exercises will be well worth it.

Each of the chapters in the book concludes with a selection of recommended publications and online resources that direct you to further reading. The selected reading is not intended to be exhaustive; however, the examples provided have been selected for their relevance and readability. At the time of writing, all website addresses were working correctly. However, website addresses are notoriously ephemeral as material is removed or, more often, the web address is changed. I provide the full title of the online resource, so that if the web address changes, the material may be found again by entering the title into a search engine.

Finally, please note that none of the content in the book overrides the institutional rules and regulations of the university where you are registered. While there is no substitute for real-world experience, research students can learn to better anticipate and prepare for the challenges and problems that inevitably arise during research projects. My hope is that this book can help the learning experience of research students, thereby improving the quality of their research training, research output and career development.

Chapter 1

The PhD research degree

Introduction

Being a PhD student is considerably different from the experience of being an undergraduate student. Undergraduate education is characterised by a reasonably well-defined curriculum for which taught classes are largely controlled or facilitated by a lecturer. The curriculum tends to focus on well-established knowledge that is the product of a research discipline. Handouts are provided, textbooks are recommended, and you are one of a group of peers participating in the same course and sharing many of the same experiences. There are several stages of assessment, and past exam papers are available that serve as a clear guide to the expected standard.

In contrast, there is no curriculum for the PhD: in effect, *you* design the curriculum for your PhD project (with assistance from your supervisor). As well as mastering the generally accepted knowledge of a research discipline, the need to undertake original research requires doctoral students to master the development and understanding of uncertain knowledge. A major feature of doctoral research is this engagement with the development of new knowledge, as well as the evaluation of uncertain and tentative knowledge.

Given that new students will be inexperienced and unaware of the nature of the PhD research degree, this chapter provides guidance on some important issues. I briefly discuss the main purpose of the PhD and relatively common issues that arise for students doing a PhD. Considerable attention is given to the standards associated with doctoral research and the requirement for doctoral research to display 'independence', 'contribution to knowledge', 'originality', and 'suitability for publication'. A final section discusses the educational benefits of doing a PhD, and how these may be expected to contribute to your professional development.

The nature of the PhD: an overview

The implicit expectation of a PhD degree is that the doctoral graduate is capable of *independently* conducting original research of a standard that is expected of professional researchers in their particular discipline. The requirement for originality and the ability to work independently make your PhD 'curriculum' a very personal and distinct entity; because of this, there can be considerable uncertainty involved as you prepare, create, focus and plan your PhD programme. However, the ability to cope with uncertainty at a personal level, and to resolve uncertainty in the design and interpretation of original research is part of becoming an independent researcher. In time, you will appreciate that the enjoyment and satisfaction derived from research are intimately associated with such efforts to identify, understand and investigate uncertainty.

Phillips and Pugh (1994: 19) discuss the nature of the PhD degree and place considerable emphasis on the doctorate as recognition that the holder is a fully professional researcher, meaning that they can do the following:

- Can produce research that is of interest to other professional researchers.
- Have a command of the subject to the extent that they can evaluate the work of other researchers.
- Are astute enough to identify where they can make a useful contribution.
- Are able to communicate their results at a level that is appropriate to an audience of professional researchers.

The ultimate aim of the award of a PhD degree, therefore, is a recognition of both your ability and status as an independent researcher, and your learning and implementation of high-level skills. Indeed, a strong implication of the emphasis on becoming a professional researcher is that the process of the PhD (learning and practice of high-level research skills) is at least as important as the product of the PhD (the research findings in the thesis). This distinction between the research training process of the PhD and the research product of the PhD is important: you need to maintain your focus on not just producing a specific piece of original, high-quality research, but also on your training and learning to be a researcher who is more generally capable of conducting original, high-quality research:

You are not doing some research for its own sake; you are doing it in order to demonstrate that you are a fully professional researcher, with a good grasp of what is happening in your field and capable of evaluating the impact of new contributions to it – your own as well as others'. That is what you get the doctorate for.

(Phillips and Pugh 1994: 60)

New PhD students commonly consider – mistakenly – the PhD to be a single great piece of work that makes a major contribution to the research discipline. Unfortunately, this perspective over-estimates what is required. In contrast, experienced researchers and supervisors place considerable emphasis on the doctoral research project being both manageable and achievable (see Chapter 3):

[T]here are two views of the PhD: a perfect small-scale piece of research study, or a worthwhile learning experience. There is a third view which students often begin with and have to be talked out of: it is a topic or a problem so complex and enormous that it would take a lifetime's work to complete.

(Lawton 1997: 8)

Supervisors are aware that it is adequate for a thesis to make an incremental contribution to knowledge and understanding – a PhD does not have to inspire a revolution in thinking about a research discipline. As one examiner put it, ' . . . A PhD is three years of solid work, not a Nobel Prize.'

(quoted in Mullins and Kiley 2002: 386)

Although Lawton (1997) distinguishes between the PhD as 'a perfect small-scale piece of research study, or a worthwhile learning experience', these two views are not mutually exclusive. Again, new students often under-estimate this view of the PhD as a learning experience; however, it is inevitable that you will have to learn and implement a variety of new skills, especially during the first year. As a personal example, most of the first year of my PhD was spent attempting to investigate the toxic effects of agricultural chemicals on beetles, however, an account of these initial experiments never appeared in my thesis. I lacked confidence in the research methods that I had originally used, largely due to the method-ological insights gained later in my doctoral research. Back then, I deeply resented the time that I had apparently 'wasted' on that work, but now appreciate that the experience and insight provided by the first year of my research prepared me to properly investigate my research questions in the second and third years.

Features of being a PhD research student

One of the major challenges when doing a PhD is that *you* are responsible for managing *your* progress. This cannot be over-emphasised. Throughout the PhD, there will be important decisions to be made. Thus, many elements of the PhD programme require your exercise of judgement on big issues (Which research questions should I focus on? What is my evaluation of others' research? What research methods should I choose? What assumptions am I making in my choice of research methods?) and on smaller ones (Where do I seek permission to use this piece of equipment? Who should attend this meeting?). Although your exercise of judgement may be challenging and demanding at times, it is also empowering, and is a hallmark of your development as an independent researcher. Of course, this is not to say that you will work in complete isolation with little or no assistance; you will have (and are entitled to) support and guidance from your supervisor and others. Ultimately, however, achieving the award of PhD degree is *your* responsibility.

One implication of such responsibility is that your motivation for undertaking a research degree is essential for your success. You will need to persevere through sometimes tedious and repetitive work and at other times some very challenging and difficult periods of study. Unfortunately, over a relatively long research period, it is also likely that you will experience some form of personal crisis, such as relationship problems, or an illness or death in the family. It may be difficult to sustain yourself through such academic and personal challenges for the duration of the PhD unless you are highly motivated and focused.

Cryer (2000: 12) indicates the following motivations that are likely to bring success:

- developing a trained mind;
- satisfying intellectual curiosity;
- finding a challenge when one feels 'in a rut';
- experiencing and engaging with an academic community;
- contributing to knowledge;
- fulfilling a lifelong ambition.

Despite (or maybe because of) the challenges, successful PhD students generally enjoy doing research and derive considerable satisfaction and reward from undertaking a doctoral research degree. They engage totally with their research topic, enjoy reading about it, and relish the opportunity to make their own contribution. To get through the difficult periods that inevitably arise, it is important that you are genuinely interested in the topic in which you will specialise for a number of years, and for which you will make many personal sacrifices:

> Be absolutely sure you love your field enough to give up time, money, effort, and sweat . . . If you're not 100% certain, then do something else for a while. It's a wonderful, exhilarating, horrible, frustrating process; you'll be poor for years, you'll work like a dog, your advisor will probably kick your ego around a bit, so if you're not passionate about your field you'll probably have a hard time. On the other hand, it can be a great experience. I'm glad I did it, but I can't say it's been easy.
>
> (PhD student, quoted in Golde 2001)

Exercise 1.1

1   Why do *you* want to do a PhD? List your reasons in order of importance.
2   What are your career plans for five and ten years time and how will a PhD degree contribute to your career development?

Expected standards of doctoral research

When you set off on a car journey, major decisions on your route are dictated by the starting point and the nature of the destination, e.g. in which direction to travel, how much time it takes to get there, how many stops to make and what your destination looks like as you approach it. Importantly, the end of the journey influences decisions that are made even *before* the journey begins. In a similar way, an understanding of the end-point of the PhD degree should influence how you embark on your research project. Thus, knowledge of the expected standards of the PhD degree will help you plan your PhD project in a way that consciously addresses such requirements. This section discusses in detail the question:

What constitutes research at doctoral level? (the 'destination' of a PhD); later chapters will look at the means by which you achieve doctoral research (the 'route').

It is essential that you know the expected standards for doctoral research if you are to adequately plan your research objectives and assess your progress. There are at least four main methods to understand the expected standard of research at doctoral level:

1   Identify the regulations and expectations as set out in formal university documents.
2   Discuss such issues with your supervisor, other academics and other PhD students.
3   Read other PhD theses in your research area (an under-used method).
4   Investigate and be aware of the criteria that PhD examiners use to assess doctoral research (see Chapter 7).

In this section, I will focus on the regulations and expected standards.

An improved understanding of the requirements for the award of Doctor of Philosophy (PhD) can be achieved by comparison with the general requirements for the award of Master of Philosophy (MPhil). Although the details vary among different universities, an MPhil usually requires the student to demonstrate an understanding of research methods appropriate to the discipline and to implement research skills necessary to carry out supervised research at a professional level. The MPhil may require originality in the application of existing knowledge, and the ability to critically evaluate current research and understanding in the discipline. The MPhil involves a shorter registration period and the thesis is typically shorter than the PhD thesis and does not have to be of a publishable standard. Overall, compared to the PhD, the MPhil is of more limited scope and less exacting in its demands for originality, depth and scope of investigation, critical evaluation and independence.

The expected standard of the PhD degree is exemplified by the following definition:

> A PhD thesis must form a distinct contribution to the knowledge of the subject and afford evidence of originality, shown by the discovery of new facts, or by the exercise of independent critical power. Additionally, a PhD thesis must show work which, if written in a suitable form, would be publishable.
>
> (modified from Cryer 2000: 186)

There are several versions of this type of definition, but key issues used when defining or discussing the expected standard of a PhD degree are 'independence', 'contribution to knowledge', 'originality', and 'suitability for publication'. In the following sections, I discuss these fundamental requirements. It is important that you discuss these issues with your supervisor (and other PhD students), in order to gain a firm understanding about how the general principles in this chapter apply to your specific research.

Independence

The PhD degree provides a learning experience such that the PhD research student will graduate as an independent researcher. Therefore, the PhD graduate is expected to be able to conduct advanced research without supervision, and be capable of identifying research questions of relevance and significance, designing an appropriate and feasible methodology to test such questions, and communicating the research findings at a level of significant scholarship.

It is expected that the PhD research and thesis are the student's own work. Of course, the supervisor has a significant role as a guide from whom a certain amount of assistance can be expected. The requirement for independence is certainly not a justification for a supervisor to neglect their responsibilities; however, there are limits to the assistance that a supervisor should provide (see Chapter 2). As an example, examiners indicated that the requirement for independence would not be upheld where the supervisor writes sections of the thesis, or directly analyses and interprets the student's data (Hockey 1997: 50). Although it is common for supervisors to have a strong guiding role in the initial stages of a project, one would have to seriously question the independence of a PhD student's work if it has been *totally* inspired and designed by the supervisor with little or no opportunity for the student to contribute; a student is almost certainly not receiving training to be an independent researcher if they are effectively being treated as a specialised research assistant.

A modern feature of research in many disciplines is an increase in larger, collaborative research projects that involve a team of researchers, including PhD students. In such cases, there may well be an overlap in some work or contributions by several individuals, but this need not necessarily clash with the requirement for independence. To clarify the situation, however, many universities request that the PhD thesis is accompanied by a statement from the student that describes the extent to which others assisted the doctoral research, with a clear description of the nature of this assistance. Such a clarification may also arise when the student includes a published paper as part of their submitted thesis (see Chapter 5).

Contribution to knowledge

Despite the widespread and important expectation that PhD research will make a distinct or significant contribution to knowledge, there is relatively little elaboration of either the nature or extent of this contribution. The nature of the contribution to knowledge will be expected to vary across disciplines; for example, the form of a contribution to knowledge will differ, depending on whether the research discipline is history, philosophy, music, politics, biology, physics or chemistry. Nevertheless, some common components of what constitutes a contribution to knowledge can be identified, which should be generally applicable. These components include the nature of the research question, the use of an effective research methodology and evidence of critical evaluation.

Nature of the research question

Not all research that can be carried out is necessarily appropriate to a doctoral research programme; research is not necessarily of a doctoral standard just because it is systematic, establishes facts or collects information. There are many reports that conduct investigations to establish facts or collect information, e.g. surveys of the number of unemployed people in geographical regions, house price comparisons, pollution levels in rivers and lakes, or smoking and drinking habits of men and women. Despite the fact that such investigations may be important, difficult to compile and complex to analyse, they would not usually be considered appropriate research topics for doctoral research.

So what exactly is it about doctoral research that is different? To make a contribution to knowledge, doctoral research is expected to work at the boundaries of knowledge, and is characterised by a contribution to the conceptual or theoretical development of a research discipline. One of the features and advantages of a theoretical basis to doctoral research is that theory facilitates the formulation of predictions and hypotheses, which become the doctoral research questions. In this way, the research contributes to an advancement in understanding. Across many disciplines, examiners (and other readers) expect doctoral research to have a strong theoretical or conceptual basis and to do the following:

identify and explain relevant relationships between the facts. In other words, the researchers must produce a concept or build a theoretical structure that can explain facts and the relationships between them . . . The importance of theory is to help the investigator summarise previous information and guide his [sic] future course of action. Sometimes the formulation of a theory may indicate missing ideas or links and the kinds of additional data required. Thus, a theory is an essential tool of research in stimulating the advancement of knowledge still further.

(Verma and Beard 1981: 10)

Thus, doctoral research questions typically investigate the relationship between variables, within the context of the conceptual or theoretical development of the discipline. In this way, doctoral research goes beyond just being a descriptive study and operates at a deeper level that seeks explanations, tests predictions and aims to extend understanding at the forefront of the discipline.

Doctoral research questions are expected to have a sense of being worthwhile, i.e. be non-trivial, but this should be relatively easy to ensure. Obviously, when doctoral research is aimed at either extending the boundaries of knowledge through a broadening of the scope of the discipline (new knowledge through new investigation) or a reorganisation of understanding associated with the existing discipline (new knowledge through critical evaluation that leads to a modified/improved interpretation of previous knowledge), then the mutual dependence between 'originality' and the 'contribution to knowledge' quickly becomes evident. A separate and more detailed discussion of originality is provided below.

Effective methodology

As you identify appropriate research questions for your doctoral research, you will also begin to consider how the research will be conducted to address these questions. This stage of research design is infused with decision-making and choices about the approaches to conducting the research. A research methodology involves a thorough reflection, identification and justification of the choice of research methods:

To be sure, there already exist traditions and 'blueprints' of practice which suggest – more or (often) less critically – ways of proceeding and which frequently condition our view of how phenomena should be investigated. But these should never be seen as techniques which can be lifted wholesale from other accounts and imported uncritically into an enquiry motivated by specifically different situations and subjects . . . Thus methodology starts quite simply by asking questions such as: 'Why interview?', 'Why carry out a questionnaire survey?', 'Why interview 25 rather than 5000 participants?'. Decisions such as these are apparently often practical, but they carry very deep, often unarticulated implications. They are often based on values and assumptions which influence the study, and as such therefore need to be fully interrogated in order to clarify the research decisions which are made.

(Clough and Nutbrown 2002: 17, 22)

Thus, you need to provide a clear explanation of the assumptions that underpin your decision-making when designing your research, some of which are explicit but, if you are not careful, more of which may be implied or assumed.

It should also be clear that 'methodology' is not the same as 'research methods'; methodological considerations aim to ensure that the chosen research methods are valid, reliable, rigorous and appropriate to the research questions. Given that you are investigating an original research question, it may well be that the most appropriate method of investigation will require the modification of an existing research method, or the design of a completely new method. Of course, no single methodology is perfect and the ability to identify the limitations associated with a particular methodology (your own, and that of others) is an important demonstration of your mastery of your research discipline. Your methodological considerations should fully identify and consider any existing limitations to interpretation that your methodology helps to overcome, as well as any remaining (or new) limitations.

The ability to carefully consider and select an appropriate research methodology is a fundamental criterion for the award of PhD degree. Your research practices should arise from an evaluation of different approaches, so that you choose *with justification* the approach that maximises the validity, reliability and appropriateness of your research methodology. For example, the examination criteria of the Institute of Education (see Box 7.1, in Chapter 7) state that:

Since determination of the most appropriate methodology is not always a straightforward matter, candidates should justify the methods chosen, with an appropriate rationale in each case . . . Potential alternative methods should be rejected on the basis of a reasoned case. Candidates should be able to demonstrate that the methods used have been chosen through a conscious process of deliberation; and that the criteria for, and advantages and disadvantages of, particular choices of method are well specified.

To summarise this section, an important outcome of a good methodology is that the reader (including an examiner) has more confidence in the validity of the design and execution of the research, and your contribution to knowledge is more convincing, persuasive and authoritative. Not surprisingly, PhD examiners place a strong emphasis on proficiency in research methodology, and methodological questions are a feature of the oral examination (Trafford and Leshem 2002; Mullins and Kiley 2002; see Chapter 7). Thus, there is an onus on you to include methodological considerations in your research planning, and to communicate clearly in the thesis how you have considered and justified your choice of methods (see Chapter 7). A written account in the PhD thesis of such considerations provides the examiners with evidence of your ability to independently conduct research.

Exercise 1.2

1   Identify the research methods of PhD theses from past students and from selected important research papers in your discipline.

2   Does the thesis communicate clearly the justification for the selection of the methods?

3   Are the methods valid, reliable and persuasive? Explain your answer.

4   In your research, what methods have you adopted? Why have you chosen these particular methods? What assumptions underpin your choices?

5   Are you confident that your chosen research methods correspond to the research objectives?

Evidence of critical evaluation

Your thesis will be examined to ensure that it contains an intellectual appreciation of the conceptual and theoretical basis of your research discipline, as well as the limitations and wider significance of the contribution to knowledge made by your research. Evidence of your intellectual appreciation and command of the subject area will be particularly evident in your critical evaluation that appears in the literature review (see Chapter 4), and the rationale that supports your identification of the doctoral research questions. Similarly, the methodological considerations that inform your selection of the appropriate research methods will be dependent on your critical evaluation. It is particularly important to identify the contribution of your research to the knowledge of the wider research discipline, e.g. how does your research relate to the existing understanding of your subject and what advances in theory, concepts or methodology has your thesis provided? The evaluation criteria suggested in Chapters 4 and 6 will provide a useful guide to evaluating the contribution of your own research to the wider research discipline. Note that although there are sections of your thesis that are more readily identifiable as a critical evaluation of the research discipline than others, the critical evaluation of your research methodology, your research findings and the wider research discipline is part of a critical research attitude that should permeate all your doctoral research.

Although the structure of a PhD thesis differs across faculties and universities, a common structure includes a lengthy introductory chapter that incorporates a literature review, and a concluding chapter in which the contribution of your research to the knowledge of the wider research discipline is identified. Individual chapters may also contain other more detailed review, description of methodology and discussion. Such sections of the thesis provide evidence of critical evaluation. Irrespective of the specific thesis structure, however, such critical evaluation must appear somewhere in your thesis.

Originality

An *original* contribution to knowledge is an especially prominent requirement for the award of a PhD degree. But what is originality? How does one develop and recognise it? How much originality should a PhD thesis possess?

In addressing these questions, it seems that 'there is little or no discussion between supervisors and students of what constitutes originality in the PhD' (Phillips and Pugh 1994: 62). Supervisors are able to judge the limitations and reasonable expectations associated with the PhD, and appreciate that it is not too difficult for research to possess originality. In contrast, students in the early stages of their doctoral research can be unsure about the magnitude of the original contribution to knowledge that is required, and may over-compensate by being far too ambitious in their research plans. If you are worried about the extent of originality in your work, discuss and clarify these issues with your supervisor. Exercise 1.3 may also improve your ability to judge these expectations for yourself.

Exercise 1.3

This exercise aims to improve your awareness of the standard, originality and contribution to knowledge that can be expected from the PhD.

1   Read some completed PhD theses from your department and identify:

- their originality
- their contribution to knowledge
- their critical evaluation.

Do the theses clearly indicate how they made an original contribution to knowledge? Where is this evident?

2   If possible, talk to other PhD students about what they consider to be the original contribution to knowledge made by their research.

3   Identify how *your* doctoral research is likely to demonstrate an original contribution to knowledge and critical evaluation.

The following discussion of originality largely relies on lecture notes provided by Michael Talbot, a retired Professor of Music at the University of Liverpool. He also provides an encouraging message for PhD students – that the achievement of originality in the PhD thesis is not as daunting or difficult as you might think:

The recognition and acceptance that originality in the PhD typically transforms into an achievable requirement should be quite reassuring to research students. Of course, flashes of inspiration are infrequent in any scholar's life. In fact, most kinds of originality do not depend on them. Originality can be built up almost by stealth, as one thing leads (normally gently) to another. It often happens that one arrives at the end of a project before one is able to take the measure of how original the contribution is, and this illustrates the point . . . that originality is a by-product of quite ordinary scholarly activity. It arises by itself, uninvited. All one has to do is to recognise it when it emerges and give it full scope.

(Talbot, pers. comm.)

This statement about originality being an achievable requirement is consistent with the view that the PhD project as a whole should be manageable and achievable. Originality may be achieved through exceptionally profound (but rare) insights; however, originality is more often achieved through 'quite ordinary scholarly activity'. When doctoral research aims to extend the boundaries of knowledge, the mutual dependence between 'originality' and the 'contribution to knowledge' is most evident: it is difficult to imagine how a contribution to knowledge at doctoral level could be made without some originality. The important point is to actively identify such originality when it occurs and to pursue and develop its contribution to your doctoral research.

Talbot highlights how originality is not dependent on moments of brilliance, but can arise from ordinary research as result of recognising research links or relationships: 'originality, nine times out of ten, is not about *invention* but about *combination*. In other words, it is about bringing together known elements that hitherto have been kept apart rather than conjuring new things out of the void' (Michael Talbot, pers. comm.). Based on a simple but useful scheme, Talbot discusses the potential for originality to arise by linking 'ideas' ('ways of marshalling the facts to produce arguments, inferences, hypotheses and conclusions') and 'facts' ('verifiable data'), and whether they are 'old' or 'new', as follows:

1   New facts + new ideas.
2   New facts + old ideas.
3   Old facts + new ideas.
4   Old facts + old ideas.

Using this example, only the last combination offers no scope for originality. Of course, this basic distinction between 'facts' and 'ideas' can be extended to include further distinctions between 'theory', 'hypotheses', 'methods' and 'facts', each of which may be old or new, e.g. old theory + new hypotheses + old methods + new facts. A specific example of how a combinatory approach contributed to originality is provided in Box 1.1.

Box 1.1 Case study of originality

Michael Talbot (pers. comm.) provides an example of originality from the work by a former PhD student of his, Paul Everett, who was interested in the analysis of the physical properties of paper used in historical musical manuscripts:

'I pointed [Paul] towards a group of articles on paper analysis that would serve as a "crash course" in bibliography. When he read them, he suddenly realised that he could apply sophisticated bibliographical techniques familiar to students of English to musical manuscripts, but developing them to take account of a special property of paper [that is] used for writing down music: the stave-lines drawn across the page. To rule these lines, one needs an instrument (a *rastrum* or *rastral*) that draws one, two, four, six, twelve or however many five-line staves one wants, in a single action. Each such instrument has its peculiar characteristics (rather like an old-fashioned typewriter), and if a given rastrum is employed only for one kind of paper, it is possible to define the music manuscript paper not in traditional terms based on dimensions, colour, thickness, watermarks and chainlines but in terms of its *rastrography*: the pattern of ruled staves (which are much more amenable to inspection than, for instance, water-marks). Within a mere month, Paul had perfected his system for identifying and classifying *rastrographies* (this term was coined by him), and, with it, the new science of *rastrology*. Today, he is a world expert in the science, and Vivaldi (and other) scholars write to him for advice and assistance.

'Where this fits in with our subject of originality is that Paul's brainwave arose from combination. The starting point was his application to musicology of an approach not ready-made but appropriated from literary bibliography. Once this breakthrough had been made, the rest was just a matter of technique and persistence.'

Some general examples of how originality may arise in doctoral research is provided in Appendix 1; note how frequently the combination of old approaches to new situations (and new approaches to old situations) features in these examples.

Suitability for publication

'Publication' usually refers to publication in a peer-reviewed journal, but can also refer to publication of the thesis as a book or research monograph. Here, I discuss the common expectation that the PhD thesis contains elements that are worthy of publication. Many universities require that a PhD thesis must contain work that is worthy of being published, some other universities have no such requirement while others make publication a formal requirement for award of the PhD degree (e.g. some universities in The Netherlands, Sweden and Eastern European countries). You should find out what the relevant regulations are at your university.

Although it may not be strictly necessary to have published any of your doctoral research before the PhD examination (where the thesis is expected to show *potential* for publication), having some of your work in press or published provides examiners with *prima facie* evidence that your work satisfies the requirement to be of publishable quality (see Chapter 6). Not all the doctoral research reported in the thesis must be worthy of publication – it is sufficient for *some* of the research to attain this standard. However, some universities specify that the quantity and quality of the thesis should be approximately equivalent to any number from one to four journal publications, depending on the university and country. In terms of developing your professional career, it may be quite important to ensure that a significant proportion of your doctoral research is publishable (see Chapter 6).

Box 1.2 Generic questions to assess doctoral standard

Trafford and Leshem (2002) identified a number of generic questions that examiners predictably ask in the oral examination (the questions are reproduced in Chapter 7). They point out that a consideration of these questions, which assess the doctoral quality in the oral examination, may also help students at the beginning of their doctoral research to better approach the design, conduct, analysis and presentation of their research throughout the duration of the PhD, in a way that *consciously achieves and demonstrates doctoral qualities*. They acknowledge the potential difficulties in trying to answer these questions, but warn that if these difficulties are not resolved, then they will appear as serious omissions, or major faults, within the submitted thesis. Although the task may be difficult, it is a necessary part of the research process and one that can remove later problems for you.

(ibid.: 48)

Educational and professional benefits of a PhD degree

A doctorate represents the culmination of higher education, so what educational benefits may be expected? You may not reflect too deeply on this in the earlier stages of the PhD programme, but these issues invariably become more important as you approach the end of your PhD. An awareness of the education and skills that you develop during your doctoral research will be invaluable when you finish your research and begin the next stage of your career.

Transformative experience

Ultimately, education is an experience of personal transformation, although the nature of the transformation varies considerably and may be intensely personal. Examples of such personal transformations include gaining a qualification, learning and developing new skills, improving employment opportunities, professional development, personal development, the pursuit of a challenge, the pleasure of learning and the advancement of knowledge. Of course, these examples are neither exhaustive nor mutually exclusive.

Specialist knowledge and skills

Traditionally, the specialist knowledge and skills developed during the PhD were seen as a preparation for a career in research or academia. It is difficult to be prescriptive, but examples might include: specialist knowledge of your subject discipline; awareness of the boundaries of knowledge within your subject discipline; an ability to describe a research problem and develop an appropriate methodology; the ability to use specialised software or technical equipment. Nevertheless, the reality nowadays is that many PhD graduates do not continue in research or academia, but enter quite different careers where they are highly successful (and desired by employers). Therefore, it should be obvious that the completion of doctoral research endows the student with more than just specialist knowledge.

Transferable skills

The completion of a postgraduate research degree typically demonstrates ability to sustain application to a research project for a substantial period of time and apply a variety of management and communication skills to an original piece of research. This should also indicate ability to successfully manage a project; to identify and resolve problems; to demonstrate initiative and determination; and to communicate to a high standard. Interviews with doctoral graduates indicated that, in their opinion, one of the most important outcomes from the PhD process is the training and development of practical and intellectual skills as much as (if not more than) the original contribution to knowledge from their research (Pole 2000).

These abilities associated with the process of getting a PhD are applicable to a wide variety of situations; hence, they are known as transferable skills. The Joint Skills Statement in Box 1.3 describes the transferable skills that a typical doctoral research student (in the UK, at least) would be expected to develop during their research training.

Box 1.3 Joint Statement of the Research Councils'/ AHRB'S Skills Training Requirements for Research Students

(A) Research skills and techniques – to be able to demonstrate:
1. The ability to recognise and validate problems.
2. Original, independent and critical thinking, and the ability to develop theoretical concepts.
3. A knowledge of recent advances within one's field and in related areas.
4. An understanding of relevant research methodologies and techniques and their appropriate application within one's research field.
5. The ability to critically analyse and evaluate one's findings and those of others.

---

6. An ability to summarise, document, report and reflect on progress.

(B) Research environment – to be able to:
1. Show a broad understanding of the context, at the national and international level, in which research takes place.
2. Demonstrate awareness of issues relating to the rights of other researchers, of research subjects, and of others who may be affected by the research, e.g. confidentiality, ethical issues, attribution, copyright, malpractice, ownership of data and the requirements of the Data Protection Act.
3. Demonstrate appreciation of standards of good research practice in their institution and/or discipline.
4. Understand relevant health and safety issues and demonstrate responsible working practices.
5. Understand the processes for funding and evaluation of research.
6. Justify the principles and experimental techniques used in one's own research.
7. Understand the process of academic or commercial exploitation of research results.

(C) Research management – to be able to:
1. Apply effective project management through the setting of research goals, intermediate milestones and prioritisation of activities.
2. Design and execute systems for the acquisition and collation of information through the effective use of appropriate resources and equipment.
3. Identify and access appropriate bibliographical resources, archives, and other sources of relevant information.
4. Use information technology appropriately for database management, recording and presenting information.

(D) Personal effectiveness – to be able to:
1. Demonstrate a willingness and ability to learn and acquire knowledge.
2. Be creative, innovative and original in one's approach to research.

3.   Demonstrate flexibility and open-mindedness.
4.   Demonstrate self-awareness and the ability to identify own training needs.
5.   Demonstrate self-discipline, motivation, and thoroughness.
6.   Recognise boundaries and draw upon/use sources of support as appropriate.
7.   Show initiative, work independently and be self-reliant.

(E) Communication skills – to be able to:
1.   Write clearly and in a style appropriate to purpose, e.g. progress reports, published documents, thesis.
2.   Construct coherent arguments and articulate ideas clearly to a range of audiences, formally and informally through a variety of techniques.
3.   Constructively defend research outcomes at seminars and viva examination.
4.   Contribute to promoting the public understanding of one's research field.
5.   Effectively support the learning of others when involved in teaching, mentoring or demonstrating activities.

(F) Networking and teamworking – to be able to:
1.   Develop and maintain co-operative networks and working relationships with supervisors, colleagues and peers, within the institution and the wider research community.
2.   Understand one's behaviours and impact on others when working in and contributing to the success of formal and informal teams.
3.   Listen, give and receive feedback and respond perceptively to others.

(G) Career management – to be able to:
1.   Appreciate the need for and show commitment to continued professional development.
2.   Take ownership of and manage one's career progression, set realistic and achievable career goals, and identify and develop ways to improve employability.

3. Demonstrate an insight into the transferable nature of research skills to other work environments and the range of career opportunities within and outside academia.
4. Present one's skills, personal attributes and experiences through effective CVs, applications and interviews.

Source: <http://www.grad.ac.uk/3_2_1.jsp>
Developed by the UK Research Councils, Arts and Humanities Research Board and UK GRAD Programme. Reproduced with permission.

Research and transferable skills may be learned in a number of ways. Some universities have dedicated taught courses that PhD students must undertake, and this is becoming more widespread. However, attendance at formal taught courses should supplement other methods, for example, self-tuition through reading relevant literature and training manuals; practising new skills; reflecting on your research and management practices; reflecting on and learning from your past experiences; tutoring by your supervisor, and learning from other postgraduate students.

Exercise 1.4

1   What transferable skills are you:

- developing?
- improving?
- mastering?

It may be useful to repeat this exercise every six to eight months, as your PhD progresses.

Networking

One of the functions of the award of the PhD degree is to acknowledge the candidate's entry as an equal to a community of scholarship. Nevertheless, your participation in the academic community should begin long before then. This community is comprised of fellow research students, more senior researchers and academic staff, both within and outside your university or research institute. Networking and engaging with other scholars and practitioners are excellent ways of exchanging information, getting feedback on your ideas and keeping up to date with new developments: 'New ideas and techniques come from using mental and technical skills in communities which value them and are producing them. In the research process the ongoing activities of others are prompts for the development of one's own work' (Francis 1997: 23).

Networking is a feature of the modern academic community, and for the PhD student it performs a number of important functions. First, finding out about the work of other researchers is an opportunity to better understand the context, originality, contribution and standard of your own research; for most students, this can be a very reassuring experience that confirms that their work is comparable to the standards of other researchers. Second, networking exposes one to professional academic discourse. The research community tends to communicate by following certain conventions and it is important for PhD students to learn to engage in such academic discourse when communicating with other researchers. As one example of academic discourse, note the blend of logic, advocacy and caution with which researchers may present a new idea: the responsible researcher provides evidence for an argument that is tempered with caveats about methodology or applicability. When you attend a presentation at a meeting or conference, note the nature of the questions and how the presenter deals with them. Questions may be very politely stated, yet extremely penetrating and rigorous. Similarly, the ways in which questions are answered can be revealing. One can learn a lot from the strategies that experienced academics use to answer questions. For example, questions may be paraphrased, qualified or split into two more distinct questions, and explanations are based on reasoned arguments. You may also encounter examples of how *not* to answer a question, but such cases are of learning value also. As another example of academic discourse, more informal discussions with researchers can explore a richer variety of viewpoints and contain more speculation than is either possible or appropriate in a public lecture. Very often, it is during these informal discussions and exchanges of ideas that academic alliances are formed, and it is an example of the importance of face-to-face meetings with other researchers. An important point is that you should aim to learn from academic discourse as performed by professional researchers because it is invaluable both when writing your thesis and when answering questions during your *viva*. The PhD oral examination is an important example of academic discourse, and being able to discuss your thesis in the manner of a professional academic is another way in which you can fulfil the expectations of the examiners. A third function of networking is its direct contribution to your career development: your interaction with other researchers may identify potential for collaborative work, which may even result in securing employment options after your PhD. For example, although relatively rare, it is not unknown for PhD students to leave a conference with an invitation to attend a job interview or an offer of a research position. Fourth, networking with others can be a powerful force for motivation, and prevents you from feeling academically isolated.

PhD students should have several opportunities for networking and interacting. Within your own institution, you have the academic interaction with your supervisor and other PhD students and there is most probably a variety of university seminars, departmental seminars, discussion groups and student presentations. Attendance at conferences and meetings of special interest groups or societies is an invaluable way of making contact with relevant researchers in other universities or research institutions. The medium of email makes it much easier to develop and maintain contacts with researchers, or to participate in electronic discussions (but beware of devoting too much time to networking and not enough to your research!).

Over the duration of your research programme, it is most likely that there will be at least one important conference that is related to your specific research area. Unfortunately, there are limited funds to provide PhD students with travel expenses to attend international meetings or conferences. Grants are often available from universities, societies and funding agencies for research students to attend conferences. Even if you cannot identify travel funds, be sure to inform your supervisor of your desire to attend a conference; in the manner of a magician pulling a rabbit from a hat, supervisors can sometimes be adept at sourcing funds to send a research student to a particularly relevant and important conference.

Conclusion

The PhD degree is awarded as evidence that the doctoral graduate is capable of independently conducting original research of a professional standard. This chapter should serve to heighten your appreciation of the required standard for the award of a PhD degree and may facilitate a more detailed and focused discussion about these issues with your supervisor. It is crucial that you understand the issues about independence, making a contribution to knowledge, originality, and suitability for publication, and that you can identify these qualities in your doctoral research. In addition to providing you with training in the process of doing research, the specialist and transferable skills associated with doctoral research also provide benefits to your educational and professional development.

Recommended reading

Publications

Phillips, E.M. and Pugh, D.S. (1994) *How to Get a PhD: A Handbook for Students and their Supervisors*, 2nd edn, Buckingham: Open University Press.
Highly recommended.

Cryer, P. (2000) *The Research Student's Guide to Success*, Buckingham: Open University Press.
Highly recommended. An extremely useful and wide-ranging treatment of the personal and academic challenges of pursuing postgraduate research.

Clough, P. and Nutbrown, C. (2002) *A Student's Guide to Methodology*, London: Sage.
See especially Chapter 2. Provides a detailed discussion of methodology set in the context of social sciences but applicable to most disciplines.

Walliman, N. (2001) *Your Research Project: A Step-by-Step Guide for the First-Time Researcher*, London: Sage.
Good introduction to a philosophical treatment of the nature of knowledge and different research approaches.

Online resources

'For Grad Students' in Science's Next Wave.
http://nextwave.sciencemag.org/grd.dtl
Highly recommended. This is a portal to a wide variety of extremely useful articles and discussions on numerous aspects related to the experience of being a PhD student. It is well worth spending time on browsing the variety of issues.

Handbook for Research Higher Degree Students, James Cook University, Australia.
http://www.jcu.edu.au/courses/handbooks/research/appendixg.html
Provides PhD guidelines that reflect differences appropriate to each faculty.

'Originality and the postgraduate student' by the Language and Learning Skills Unit, University of Melbourne.
http://www.services.unimelb.edu.au/llsu/resources/pg003.html

'A PhD in just over a year and a half . . . ' by Frank Wareing.
http://www.missendencentre.co.uk/PhD1.pdf

'Network your way into work', by Dick van Vlooten.
http://nextwave.sciencemag.org/cgi/content/full/2003/12/11/3
An entertaining and insightful article on principles of networking.

Chapter 2

You and your supervisor

Introduction

The academic relationship between students and supervisors is an important one that may last long after the duration of the research degree. You and your supervisor will work together over a period of at least three years, so it is important that you have a good working relationship that is based on mutual respect, trust and understanding. Throughout your PhD project, your supervisor will be a key figure as an intellectual guide, research mentor, career guide, a source of administrative information and an interface with the formal university procedures. Unfortunately, many students only have vague ideas of what they can expect from their supervisor (and what their supervisor can expect from them). For example, students who under-estimate the expected contribution from their supervisor will not avail themselves of the assistance that they are entitled to (and for which they pay fees . . .), while students who over-estimate their supervisor's contribution will be misguided in expecting an excessive level of assistance. In both cases, such ambiguity is a recipe for misunderstanding, frustration or even conflict.

To get the most out of the student/supervisor relationship, you need to be clear on the nature and extent of the duties and expectations associated with both roles in the student/supervisor relationship. Here, the relationship between student and supervisor is discussed, with an examination of the academic duties of both the supervisor and research student. Some strategies are suggested to improve communication between you and your supervisor, and some of the issues and problems that may arise are discussed.

Responsibilities of students and supervisors

The National Postgraduate Committee (NPC) in the United Kingdom provides a number of guideline documents that contain very useful further information (www.npc.org.uk/essentials/publications). Their publication *Guidelines on Codes of Practice for Postgraduate Research* (NPC 1992) makes recommendations on the relationship of research students to their supervisors and their departments. For example, it indicates the responsibilities of the supervisors, students and those responsible for research students at the departmental level. The NPC (1995) has also published *Guidelines on Accommodation and Facilities for Postgraduate Research*, which makes recommendations on the needs of research students for office space, facilities and to be part of the academic community in their department.

If you are to develop a harmonious relationship with your supervisor, then it is essential that you fully appreciate the responsibilities of you and your supervisor: 'there should be understanding, from the inception of the relationship, of the conventions by which it is to operate' (NPC 1992). An understanding of such conventions may be helpful in reducing dissatisfaction that may arise due to a mismatch between the expectations of the supervisor and those of the student. As early as possible in your supervisory meetings, you should try and discuss such responsibilities and expectations with your supervisor (see Exercise 2.1 for further discussion). It may also be useful to discuss such issues with other PhD students.

Many institutions now have Codes of Practice or other similar documents that try to clarify the conventional responsibilities of students and supervisors, and I provide an example here. The details will differ among institutions, and such guidelines may not be exactly or entirely suited to every discipline or every student/supervisor relationship; however, they are indicative of the main issues, and should provide a basis for further discussion between you and your supervisor.

What are the responsibilities of a supervisor?

Although this is a fundamental question, it is difficult to find a prescriptive answer. Nevertheless, a selection of the most important duties of a supervisor would typically include the following:

1   Giving guidance on:

    (a) induction;

    (b) the nature of the research and the standard expected;

  (c) the planning of the research programme;
  (d) the nature and extent of the help the student may expect in preparing a thesis in its final form for submission;
  (e) literature and training courses;
  (f) attendance at taught classes, where appropriate;
  (g) requisite techniques (including arranging for training where necessary);
  (h) necessary safety precautions;
  (i) publication of the research.

2 Having relevant expertise to supervise the research degree. In some cases, a co-supervisor may be required to bring relevant expertise to the project. In such cases, the allocation of supervisory responsibilities between supervisors should be clearly defined and communicated to the student.

3 Maintaining contact with the student through regular tutorial and seminar meetings, in accordance with institutional policy and in the light of discussion with the student.

4 Being accessible to the student at other appropriate times when advice may be needed.

5 Giving advice on the necessary completion dates of successive stages of the work so that the whole thesis may be submitted within the scheduled time.

6 Requesting written work as appropriate, and returning such work with feedback in a reasonable period of time.

7 Arranging, as appropriate, for the student to talk about their research to staff at graduate seminars or conferences.

8 Writing reports on the student's progress.

9 Ensuring that the student is made aware of inadequacy of progress or of standards of work below that generally expected.

10 Actively introducing the student to researchers and events in the academic community, e.g. conferences and meetings of learned societies.

11 Informing the student of the institutional regulations concerning the oral examination, e.g. nomination procedures for the examiners, and appeals procedures.

(Source: Modified from The University of Reading 2004)

What are the responsibilities of a research student?

The duties of the student typically include:

1 Planning and discussing with the supervisor the research topic and timetable for the research.
2 Discussing with the supervisor the type of guidance and feedback that are most helpful, and agreeing a schedule of meetings.
3 Taking the initiative in raising problems or difficulties, however elementary they may seem. This includes taking the initiative in arranging meetings.
4 Agreeing and observing any necessary safety precautions.
5 Maintaining the progress of the work in accordance with the stages agreed with the supervisor, in particular including the presentation of written materials (usually in word-processed or typed form) as required in sufficient time to allow for feedback and discussion before proceeding to the next stage.
6 Drafting and circulating the agenda and support documents in advance of meetings, and drafting and circulating the minutes of meetings.
7 Keeping systematic records of work completed, and providing written progress reports.
8 Showing all supervisors the final version of the thesis in plenty of time to receive feedback before submission.
9 Deciding when they wish to submit the thesis within the prescribed period of registration, taking due account of the supervisor's opinions.

(Source: Modified from The University of Reading 2004)

The most important responsibility of a student is to *take the initiative* in relation to a variety of these issues. You are expected to be a competent researcher, who organises and manages a range of project activities at a professional level. This includes being responsible for organising meetings with your supervisor, and informing your supervisor of problems that affect your progress.

Exercise 2.1

This exercise helps you to consider your responsibilities as a PhD student, and your expectations of your supervisor.

continued

> 1   What level of support and guidance do you expect from your
>   PhD supervisor? For example, practical assistance in the
>   lab/field, frequency of meetings, reporting methods, depth of
>   feedback and feedback method (oral or written), authorship
>   of publications arising from your research, etc.
> 2   What does your supervisor expect from you?
> 3   Are your expectations reasonable?
> 4   What will you do if these expectations are not fulfilled?

The supervisor–student relationship

Although set within the more formalised conventions and responsibilities that may appear in Codes of Practice, the relationship between students and supervisors is also an interpersonal one. The following section provides an overview of some of the relationships that may arise between students and supervisor, beginning with a more abstract consideration of the topic before including some more practical issues that may arise.

Sociological research indicates, not surprisingly, that the supervisor–student relationship is a complex and varied one. Brown and Atkins (1988) described eleven roles for the supervisor as director, facilitator, adviser, teacher, guide, critic, freedom giver, supporter, friend, manager and examiner. Brown and Atkins also described a variety of possible relationships between supervisors and students:

Supervisor	Student
Director	Follower
Master	Servant
Guru	Disciple
Teacher	Pupil
Expert	Novice
Guide	Explorer
Project manager	Team worker
Auditor	Client
Editor	Author
Counsellor	Client
Doctor	Patient
Senior partner	Junior professional
Colleague	Colleague
Friend	Friend

With such a multitude of possible roles and relationships (and there are many more facets to these), it is little wonder that individual supervisor–student relationships can be so distinctive. It may also explain why students and supervisors may sometimes have different expectations of the supervisor–student relationship. To help avoid such differences, both you and your supervisor should discuss your expectations from the supervisory process. Among the variety of supervisor–student relationships listed above, you will see some that are more nurturing and supportive (guide–explorer, expert–novice), some where there is an obvious distribution of power and authority (master–servant, auditor–client), and others where there is a balanced relationship (colleague–colleague). An understanding of the variety of student/supervisor relationships may help you recognise and perhaps influence the roles that you and your supervisor adopt.

Exercise 2.2

This exercise encourages you to consider the nature of your supervisor–student relationship.

Read the different supervisor–student relationships described by Brown and Atkins (see above) and consider the following questions:

1   Which of these roles and relationships do you think are most desirable? Explain your choices.
2   In your opinion, which of the above supervisory roles best describes your relationship with your supervisor?
3   Which of the other supervisor–student relationships relate to your situation?
4   Can you identify advantages and disadvantages of these roles and relationships?
5   How might the nature of your supervisor–student relationship change over time?

Supervisory practices

Hockey (1997) reported a study of the supervisory process, resulting from interviews with eighty-nine PhD supervisors in the UK. An analysis of supervisor's responses identified a number of practices central to the effective supervision of research degrees. Although the interviews were with supervisors working in the social sciences, the issues and practices raised in the study appear to be applicable to supervisors across most other research disciplines. The findings of the study are a useful insight into the kind of support that supervisors deem to be important and are summarised below:

- *Balancing*. Supervisors face a tension between some of their roles; in particular they need to balance their responsibilities as both guide and critic:

  > On the one hand, supervisors are supposed to tender guidance on the student's academic endeavours, to suggest feasible pathways through the morass of literature, mounds of theory and what are often, to the novice researcher, formidable practical problems of original research. However, on the other hand, somewhat paradoxically, supervisors are also charged with being the student's first line examiner and are required to ensure that their charges produce material which meets the standards of a doctoral thesis.
  >
  > (Hockey 1997: 49)

- *Foreseeing*. Described as the ability to assess accurately certain kinds of possibilities within the process of the research degree study. For example, the supervisor ascertains the suitability of a student applicant for the intellectual, analytical and fieldwork requirements to conduct a research degree. The supervisor also judges the feasibility of the project.
- *Timing*. The supervisor assesses the feasibility of the projected work schedule, assesses the timing and duration of component activities of the project and monitors the student's progress. The supervisor may also match supervisory input with students' needs over the duration of the project. For example, supervisors have more frequent meetings with students at the beginning of the project (to focus on planning) and again at the end of the project (to focus on completion).
- *Critiquing*. According to Hockey:

  > The supervisor's aim is to cultivate or even enforce rigour upon the student's intellectual thinking and writing . . . The process

of critiquing . . . involves a logical dissection of ideas, and a relentless pointing out of ways in which these ideas may become more precise, analytical and thus powerful in serving the research objective.

(1997: 56)

• *Informing*. Supervisors inform students of the practical activities which occur during the research process, focusing on issues such as methodology, data handling and interpretation, writing, the presentation of the thesis and the emotional experiences associated with a prolonged research project.
• *Guiding*. Hockey (1997) distinguished between intellectual guidance and career guidance. The intellectual guidance contributes to enhancing the rate of progress, indicating the quality of research that is desirable and expected, and providing feedback and reassurance to ensure that the expected quality is attained. Supervisors also provide career guidance:

> they saw it as part of their responsibility to introduce [research students] to certain kinds of understandings, practice and opportunities which are integral to the occupational culture of academics, and which are important to the effective pursuit of a career.

(ibid.: 60)

In practice this may involve, for example, encouraging students to become involved in attending seminars, conferences and workshops. It also involves assisting the student in networking with other colleagues and academics (see Chapter 1).

These practices are relevant to students for several reasons. First, an awareness of the supervisory practices that supervisors are supposed to provide will help the student to ensure that they receive them. Second, research students also need to undertake some of these practices (foreseeing, timing, critiquing and informing) or understand these issues (balancing and guiding). In effect, these practices are important components of project management for *both* the student and supervisor. Supervisors have more experience of these practices and should be in a better position to guide the student's judgement. However, the availability of the supervisor's advice and guidance is not a substitute for the student's own efforts to manage and assess their progress.

An important practical issue for both students and supervisors is the amount of assistance that research students can expect from their supervisor. Reflecting the 'balancing' that supervisors undertake, supervisors must decide how much guidance and support they can provide to students without transgressing institutional requirements (and academic tradition) that the thesis is the student's own work. The following indicates how supervisors attempt to achieve this balance:

> Aid which actively solved [particular intellectual] problems was viewed as a violation of student responsibility and beyond the limit. [For an example of boundary-making decisions] . . . supervisors would point their students in the general direction of relevant literature, but they would not provide them with a comprehensive list of sources they should read. Moreover, they would aid students with data analysis by illustrating a particular statistical technique, but they would not actually manipulate the students' data. They would therefore illustrate or explain general cases, but not the particular.
>
> (ibid.: 50)

Probably in recognition that no individual supervisor can possess the full spectrum of academic expertise and research skills, many institutions now have thesis committees (or a group with some similar name). This committee usually comprises of a small number of research staff that brings different skills and perspectives to the research project. Typically they meet to assess and give feedback on the student's progress. If there is a thesis committee, ensure that you know the extent of its duties and responsibilities. For example, how often will the committee meet and (where appropriate) will it contribute to a decision on your upgrading from MPhil to PhD?

Communicating with your supervisor

Your academic supervisor has a very important role in advising you on how best to make progress during your research. Therefore, you need to ensure that there is sufficient and effective communication between you and your supervisor. It is difficult to suggest an optimal amount of communication (e.g. frequency and duration of meetings), and some students require more than others. Of course, there is also a significant difference between the quantity and quality of communication that can occur. This section provides some strategies and practical suggestions for making the most of communication between you and your supervisor.

Achieving more effective communication with your supervisor

Although your doctoral project dominates your time and efforts, your project is just one of many of your supervisor's commitments (see Figure 2.1). Understanding the relatively small proportion of your supervisor's time that can be devoted to your thesis should encourage you to maximise your benefit from this time. In particular, it is essential that you make the best use of the face-to-face meetings with your supervisor.

So, how do you make the most of your communication with your supervisor? The following points in Box 2.1 outline some practical suggestions about how to develop and maintain effective communication with your supervisor.

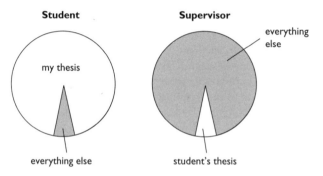

Figure 2.1 Proportional relevance of thesis to student and supervisor

---

Box 2.1 Practical suggestions to maintain communi-cation with your supervisor

1. *Discuss your expectations of your supervisor, and your supervisor's expectations of you.*
Unfortunately, students can experience dissatisfaction with the level of communication that exists between them and their supervisor. There can be many reasons for this, but a common one is that the research student lacks the confidence or ability to maintain regular, meaningful communication. This can be compounded by a supervisor who assumes that the student is making progress ('no news is good news') and is too busy to check.

Whatever the reasons, there is little doubt that ineffective communication leads to ineffective supervision. It is important to establish mutually acceptable patterns of communication and supervision early in the PhD research programme. Neither you nor your supervisor is a mind reader, so the only way to do this is to discuss the expectations that you each have. The earlier that such a discussion occurs the better, so that bad habits do not become established. Some examples of issues for discussion include: expected attendance patterns; the frequency and duration of meetings; the level of preparation for meetings (agendas, minutes); reporting and feedback practices; publication and authorship expectations.

Probably reflecting the power imbalance that exists between supervisors and students, you may feel awkward about raising such issues. Indeed, you will probably need to use a mixture of assertiveness and diplomacy in such initial discussions. (Ultimately, however, it is your research degree. You will be the one who is judged in the oral examination; therefore, you must take and maintain responsibility for your research and its management.) It may help to preface such a discussion by explaining that you would like the supervisor's advice on some issues that you recognise as being important. Most supervisors will interpret your initiative as a sign of your professional approach and conscientious management of your research project.

2. *Make appointments to see your supervisor.*
Your supervisor is likely to be a busy person, with many other commitments. Some supervisors may have an 'open door' policy; however, for most, it is always advisable to make an appointment, as opposed to turning up unannounced. When you want a meeting, email or phone your supervisor with alternative dates and times when you are available. It is a good idea to discuss these approaches to arranging a meeting with your supervisor and agree on the most mutually convenient method.

3. *Bring a written list of the issues to be discussed.*
Writing a list of the main issues for discussion will focus your mind on the main issues, help you to ask better questions, and thus help you to get the best feedback and advice. Such a list will serve as an

agenda, and keep the discussion focused. Even better, give the list to your supervisor before the meeting, which allows them time to prepare and to give the issues more thought. When you have a problem to resolve, try and bring some different solutions to the meeting. Although you may have done so many times before, be prepared to brief your supervisor on progress to date – the issues that seem familiar to you may not be so familiar to your supervisor. After the meeting, both the written list of issues and your notes will be a useful record of the agreements reached during the meeting.

4. *At the end of the meeting, agree on goals and indicate a date for the next meeting.*
You should try to finish each meeting with agreement on the short-term goals to be addressed before the next meeting. After the meeting, use your notes to make a clear (written) statement about these goals, and submit a copy to your supervisor. At the end of a meeting, fix a time and date for the next meeting, if possible; otherwise, at least try and get a clear indication of whether you expect to meet again after a period of days or weeks.

5. *Submit written work in good time, if you want to get useful feedback.*
When you submit work, make it clear that you are requesting feedback, and by what date you wish the feedback to be provided. When there are deadlines involved, ensure that you submit written work in reasonable time. If there is a lot of material, it is a good idea to let your supervisor know in advance so that he/she can schedule the time required to review your work. More detailed discussion on feedback is provided in Chapter 5.

Project meetings

Effective communication is an important characteristic of successful research projects, and may take the form of phone calls, emails, letters and written reports or face-to-face meetings. The previous section makes clear the importance of face-to-face meetings with your supervisor, and most students will rely on supervisory meetings for guidance when making strategic decisions about their research. Some broader issues that relate to supervisory meetings are discussed here.

Informal meetings

Meetings vary in nature from the very informal to the very formal. Informal meetings tend to be unscheduled, of short duration and have no written agenda. They might consist of a quick chat between you and your supervisor at which you may request your supervisor to sign an order for equipment, arrange a longer meeting or briefly inform your supervisor about a specific issue. This type of meeting may be the result of a chance meeting along a corridor, a quick encounter over coffee, or a short visit to see to your supervisor in their office. While informal, such meetings can be quite frequent and may be important in informing your supervisor's perceptions about your progress. In the absence of any other information, many supervisors will (rightly or wrongly) simply take it for granted that you have no problems.

Let's assume that this is not the case; in such an event, be sure to send a clear signal to your supervisor that all is not well. When asked 'How are you?' in a social setting, conventions in many societies expect one to provide a positive reply, such as 'Fine' or 'Never better!' It should be obvious that such a reply sends a signal to your supervisor (incorrectly, in this case) that you are getting along just fine. This is less of a problem for students who regularly meet with their supervisor and can discuss their progress in a meaningful way, as there is an opportunity to correct any false impressions. On the other hand, for students who see their supervisor less frequently, informal meetings should be used as an opportunity to communicate the existence of problems. In the context of an informal meeting, it may be inappropriate to provide a detailed breakdown of a problem. However, when asked 'How are you?', it should suffice to say something such as 'Well, I could be better. I am having quite a bit of trouble with . . . (whatever the issue is)', or 'I'm glad you asked, because I really need to arrange a meeting with you to discuss my latest research.'

Occasionally, informal meetings may develop into a longer conversation that discusses details of the progress of the project. This is valuable as a means of informing your supervisor of progress; however, be careful when an informal meeting starts making strategic decisions about the project, or is making changes to previous decisions. It is likely that you will not be properly prepared for such a discussion, and you may find yourself agreeing with decisions that you may be unsure of later on. Therefore, even if you fully support these decisions, it is important to write a short, dated report that describes the changes (and their consequences), and to give these to your supervisor as a record of the agreed decisions. If, during the meeting, you are even slightly unsure about agreeing to changes to the research project, it is preferable to summarise (verbally) the issues and ask your supervisor for time to think about these. Then schedule a formal meeting to discuss the issues more thoroughly. This should give you time to write out the proposed changes, reflect on the proposed decisions and their consequences, and consider alternative options. Only then can you make the decision that is in the best interest of your PhD project.

Formal meetings

Another particularly important form of communication is the more formal project meeting in which proposals are discussed and decisions are made. These meetings tend to be scheduled in advance, are of a reasonably long duration (30–90 minutes) and should have an agreed agenda. I refer to these as formal meetings because they represent a formal occasion within the management of your project; however, these meetings may vary in nature from a discussion over a cup of coffee to a much more official occasion at which other academics and representatives of a funding agency may attend. Regardless of the environment in which they occur, formal project meetings are extremely important and influential events in the management of your PhD project. Such meetings are important for defining the project, clarifying research questions and methodologies, considering different alternatives, proposing changes, achieving consensus, making decisions and reviewing progress. Not all of these activities may occur at a single meeting, and some of these activities are more likely to occur at particular stages of the project than others. Nevertheless, it should be clear that the time devoted to project meetings has a disproportionate influence on the strategic direction of the project. For this reason, it is crucial that you (and your supervisor) are properly prepared for meetings.

The protocol of the meeting

Meetings between you and your supervisor will tend to settle into a routine that you are both comfortable with (which is why you should adopt good habits from the beginning). However, meetings that involve other people will probably adopt a more defined protocol that is associated with more official meetings, such as meetings with your thesis committee, funding agency or upgrading committee. For the purposes of this section, I assume that people other than your supervisor are present; such meetings of a more official nature tend to adopt a protocol or convention that can be off-putting when it is encountered for the first time. Here, I provide a brief and general overview of some elements of the protocol associated with more formal meetings (you may also attend such meetings that do not directly affect your doctoral research).

Some time before a meeting is held, a provisional agenda is distributed by the chairman, perhaps by either email or letter, that lists a number of topics to be discussed at the meeting. The agenda is a very important document that allows participants to prepare for the issues to be discussed and to focus the objectives of the meeting. The agenda typically indicates the location and date of the meeting, indicates who is invited to attend and who is the chairman. Meetings typically begin with an opportunity to comment on or clarify the minutes of the previous meeting, which are usually circulated with the agenda. As an example, such comments or clarifications allow participants to correct any errors, or to request additional explanation of an issue. The remaining agenda items focus on the issues that are the primary content of the meeting. Each item may be associated with the name of the person who proposed the agenda item (and will presumably lead the discussion), and perhaps an indication of the time to be allocated to the item.

During meetings where there are several people present, you will sometimes have to work up a little courage and confidence to speak up. It may help to quickly jot down your question or comment, so that you can refer to it if necessary. And remember, you don't have to be the most eloquent speaker in the room – you only have to get your point across.

Preparing for meetings

Decisions taken at project meetings about your research are likely to have major impacts on the direction and emphasis of your research programme; therefore, it is crucial that you are prepared for meetings. If you are not prepared, you will not feel able to make a useful contribution and decisions may be made that conflict with your own plans or vision for your research. Worse still, you may not fully appreciate the ramifications of such decisions until after the meeting; however, your lack of objection during the meeting will be interpreted as support for a decision. To stress the point, adequate preparation and reflection on agenda items before the meeting will help you to anticipate and recognise such difficulties if they cannot be avoided.

Further information on meetings is available at http://www.effective meetings.com/ and http://www.mapnp.org/library/grp_skll/meetings/ meetings.htm. Exercise 2.3 provides some prompts that may help you to prepare for meetings.

Exercise 2.3

This exercise helps you to prepare for meetings of a more official nature (and those with your supervisor) through a consideration of major issues associated with the organisation and conduct of meetings.

- Has an agenda been circulated?
- Who is attending?
- Is a chairman required? If so, who will chair the meeting?
- Do I understand all the agenda items?
- Do I have an opinion on all items on the agenda?
- Have I read the minutes of the last meeting?
- What protocol will be adopted during the meeting – very formal or not?
- Am I expected to discuss or contribute to a particular item on the agenda?
- Am I expected to make a presentation?
- Is it appropriate and in my best interest to initiate a request to make a presentation or to distribute a short report in advance of the meeting?
- What outcomes do I expect from this meeting?
- What outcomes do I prefer to achieve from this meeting? Why?
- What outcomes do I not want from this meeting? Why?
- Do I expect any other attendees to disagree with or support my views?
- What time is the meeting?
- Where is the meeting?
- Do I know exactly in which building and in which room the meeting will be held?
- If I am making a presentation, what audio-visual facilities are available? Do I know who to contact if there should be a problem with the presentation facilities?
- Who will keep notes and circulate a written record?
- Who will keep a file of the minutes?

Problems with supervision

A variety of problems may arise when supervisors or students blatantly disregard their responsibilities. Even when both parties have the best of intentions, problems can and do arise in supervisor–student relationships. Interpersonal interactions almost always pose difficulties of some sort, and it would be surprising if some difficulties did not arise over a three-year period. As with any interpersonal relationship, it is worth stressing that the supervisor–student relationship is subject to the limitations that all professional, interpersonal relationships may encounter. Supervisors are human too and you should realise that they have their strengths and weaknesses. The management of research can sometimes seem easy compared to the management of interpersonal relationships. However, many such difficulties should resolve themselves satisfactorily; others may not. It is also worth remembering that many supervisors never receive any relevant training for such a responsible role. While this does not excuse inadequate supervision, it may help explain it.

Identifying supervisory problems

Problems encountered by research students include the following:

- The supervisor provides an inadequate level of feedback. This is a common complaint (see Chapter 5 for some suggestions).
- Poor quantity and quality of communication.
- Occasional arguments.
- Clash of personalities.
- Supervisor is not interested in the student's research.
- The supervisor does not know what a PhD requires.
- The supervisor has inadequate experience as a supervisor.
- The supervisor has inadequate experience as a researcher.
- The supervisor publishes the student's work without listing the student as an author.
- The supervisor treats the student as an efficient or specialised research assistant, thereby depriving them of a full training to be an independent researcher (Phillips and Pugh 1994: 25; Plevin 1996: 46).
- Bullying, intimidation or sexual harassment (specific institutional procedures will usually be in place to deal with these very serious issues).

Plevin (1996: 46) identifies a number of problems that may arise from a supervisor's 'desire to publish and gain prestige in their own fields':

- Supervisors do not allocate the necessary time for training and supervision.
- Students are treated as slave labour.
- Supervisors put too much pressure on students to produce papers.
- Supervisors do not involve the student in the production of papers.
- Supervisors push students into more topical areas of research where the supervisors have no expertise.
- Towards the end of the project, supervisors may insist on additional work being conducted. This may be to produce more publications from a successful research project, but at the expense of the student's scheduled completion and submission of the thesis. Alternatively, a supervisor may insist on additional work to compensate for earlier inadequate research, 'and they blame the shortcomings on the student rather than on their own neglect' (ibid.: 46). Of course, there are other situations where, despite the best efforts of the supervisor, students either do produce inadequate research or may need to conduct some additional work to be confident of attaining the expected standard.

The issues identified in this section are certainly not intended to portray supervisors as a bad lot. On the contrary, the majority of academics are diligent and conscientious supervisors. Others require only a small amount of nudging by their students to fully deliver their supervisory commitments. However, there is a very small minority who engage in some of the undesirable or unprofessional practices listed above.

Projects with multiple supervisors

When there is more than one supervisor, there are additional dimensions to the relationship between student and supervisor. Most often, these additional dimensions are only beneficial, with the co-supervisors bringing their combined expertise to the project.

Occasionally, having more than one supervisor brings a few extra challenges that may be easily overcome. For example, before making decisions, the student may have to evaluate two or more perspectives that are somewhat different. (This is similar to the old witticism about how a person with one clock knows the time, while a person with two clocks is never sure . . .) On a more pragmatic level, it may be more difficult to organise meetings between two supervisors who both have busy schedules. Other problems include a diffusion of responsibility, provision of conflicting advice, the student playing supervisors off against one another and the lack of an overall academic view (Phillips and Pugh 1994: 110). Unfortunately, there may be rare occasions when multiple supervision results in severe problems. For example, supervisors may have personality clashes that lead to heated arguments or to a lack of any communication (see below). Usually, the benefits of co-supervision far outweigh the occasional inconvenience, and overcoming such relatively minor challenges and inconveniences is an opportunity to develop your skills in management, teamwork and diplomacy!

Generally, when you have more than one supervisor, it is advisable to do the following:

- Maintain contact with the supervisors by holding a joint meeting at the beginning of the project and at least once a year thereafter. Ensure that they have further telephone communication at least once a term (Phillips and Pugh 1994: 111), and regular, scheduled email contact (especially if one of the supervisors is based at another university/research institute).
- Ensure that each supervisor has an up-to-date copy of the project plan (an outline of the research activities, tasks and project schedule).
- Ensure that the project plan outlines the scope of the contribution by each supervisor and indicates the area of the research programme for which each supervisor is responsible.
- Copy each supervisor with all significant correspondence, i.e. instead of sending an important document to one supervisor only, send it to each supervisor even if you only expect one of them to respond.
- Inform each supervisor of any changes to protocols, experimental designs, schedules, etc.

Addressing supervisory problems

Having attempted an overview of the problems that research students encounter, I hope that you may at least recognise these issues if they affect you. The specific nature of such problems makes it difficult to provide general advice. However, when trying to deal with such issues, some broad advice may help. First, some issues can be resolved simply by sitting down with your supervisor and discussing them, albeit with some diplomacy and tact, e.g. the quality of feedback and frequency of meetings.

For more serious issues, you need to proceed more tentatively. It depends on the issue, but in most cases it is only fair to first point out the problem to the supervisor, who then has the opportunity to respond and either change their practice or justify their position. If problems persist or threaten the quality of your project, then you need to speak to an appropriate person. Sources of help include the departmental coordinator for research projects (or equivalent), the head of department, other people with relevant responsibility for postgraduate students or the students' union. Ultimately, it may be necessary to request a change of supervisor, although this is certainly not a decision to be taken lightly. Most universities have procedures to arrange a change of supervisor for cases where the supervisor–student relationship is not working.

Exercise 2.4

1   Having read this section, can you identify any problems or issues that you need to discuss with your supervisor?
2   List the *positive* contributions that your supervisor makes to your PhD project.

Conclusion

As soon as possible, discuss with your supervisor your expectations of their supervision and the PhD project. Various sections in this book highlight the important role that your supervisor plays in guiding your decision-making and progress – therefore, effective supervision is dependent on effective communication between you and your supervisor.

Recommended reading

Publications

Cryer, P. (2000) *The Research Student's Guide to Success*, Buckingham: Open University Press.
See Chapter 7 'Interacting with your supervisor(s)'.

Murray, R. (2002) *How to Write a Thesis*, Maidenhead: Open University Press.

See the relevant section in Chapter 2 for a discussion of both the relationship between student and supervisor, and the provision of feedback by your supervisor in a way that meets your needs.

Phillips, E.M. and Pugh, D.S. (1994) *How to Get a PhD: A Handbook for Students and their Supervisors*, 2nd edn, Buckingham: Open University Press.
See Chapter 8 'How to manage your supervisor'.

Online resources

'Improving Ph.D. student mentoring takes time – do we have it?' by R. Metzke.
http://nextwave.sciencemag.org/cgi/content/full/2002/04/18/6
See also the references at the end of this article.

'The missing links' by John Wakeford.
http://education.guardian.co.uk/higher/postgraduate/story/0,12848,1169926,00.html
Provides accounts of students unhappy with their supervision.

'Nowhere to turn' by John Wakeford.
http://education.guardian.co.uk/egweekly/story/0,5500,557465,00.html
Some accounts of unsuccessful PhD students.

'Hard lessons' by John Wakeford.
http://education.guardian.co.uk/egweekly/story/0,5500,1037960,00.html
An article about unhappy international PhD students.

Chapter 3

Project management

Introduction

New research students are faced with a considerable amount of project management, yet they may have little prior experience and almost certainly no training in this important research skill. Upon beginning a PhD programme, most students know that they will 'do research', i.e. they are aware of the expectation that they will design a research programme, conduct research, interpret the collected information, and write a thesis. In addition to this conventional understanding of 'doing research' during a PhD, however, there are many other activities that underpin the organisation and successful completion of a PhD programme. For example, you will very likely need to: plan and co-ordinate the strategic aims, timing and duration of your research tasks; manage your work, time and progress; develop a variety of research skills; plan your career development, and; communicate your findings to the wider research community (see also Box 1.3). Thus, it should be obvious that there is more to a PhD project than 'doing research'; there are additional and significant requirements to define, plan, organise and control a variety of activities. A systematic approach to these activities is generally defined within the area of project management.

Project management as a research tool

The high quality of research expected at doctoral level is underpinned by your imagination, inspiration, motivation and intellect: without these, you cannot make an original contribution to knowledge (see Chapter 1). At the other extreme, an over-abundance of imagination, inspiration, motivation and intellect may provide an undefined and incoherent outpouring that is impossible to marshal into a specific and manageable research effort. Thus, there is a tension between creative forces and the pragmatic demands of rigorous research standards. In two very different examples, this tension between creativity and discipline is evident in the following:

> The price of freedom for all musicians, both composers and interpreters, is tremendous control, discipline and patience; but perhaps not only for musicians. Do we not all find freedom to improvise, in all art, in all life, along the guiding lines of discipline?
>
> (Menuhin 1972: 46)

> In the end, analysis is but an aid to the judgement and intuition of the decision-maker.
>
> (Kerzner 2003: 82)

A project management approach can help provide 'the guiding lines of discipline' and 'analysis' that direct and channel the creative effort that is necessary to support the intellectual demands of research of a doctoral standard. As such, project management is a research tool that helps translate your creativity into an effective approach to (a) develop clarity on the strategic objectives of your project; and (b) assist your achievement of the strategic objectives.

This chapter describes and discusses a variety of issues that relate to project management. Throughout the detail, it is always worth remembering that project management is a research tool and, as with any unfamiliar tool, it may take some time and practice before you learn to properly apply it to your needs. However, it is a tool that should *serve* your needs, rather than confound them; different people have different needs and their use of project management techniques will also necessarily differ. Therefore, what is probably most important in this chapter is that you appreciate the strategic approach to research that can be fostered by adopting the principles of project management.

In the remainder of this chapter, I describe and discuss the role of project management as an important part of successfully planning and conducting research, and assessing the progress of a project. The whole subject of project management encompasses a wide variety of skills and abilities, and has become an applied discipline in its own right. This chapter introduces some of the basic principles of project management that are applicable to research projects. The chapter concludes with a discussion of responsible conduct in research, with some examples of negligence and misconduct.

Project management in doctoral research

Project management: an introduction

People typically associate project management with the very lengthy, expensive and technically demanding projects such as the construction of spacecraft, bridges or rail systems. However, the very same principles that are used so successfully in larger projects can also be applied to much smaller projects – including your PhD. Indeed, many (if not most) funding agencies and research institutions use fundamental principles of project management both to evaluate research proposals and to monitor the progress of funded projects. This reliance on project management in both the academic and industrial research communities illustrates that knowledge of project management techniques is an important transferable skill and is yet another reason for you to understand and implement these practices in your own research.

Project management: basic principles

For simplicity, I will indicate some of the basic principles of project management that are most relevant in the context of PhD projects. An explanation of some basic terminology is provided in Table 3.1. A typical definition of project management describes it as 'a discipline of combining systems, techniques, and people to complete a project within established goals of time, budget and quality' (Baker and Baker 2000). Definitions of projects and their management place a clear emphasis on three inter-related elements of projects:

- cost (available finance);
- quality (the expected standard of the PhD degree);
- time (the duration, milestones and deadlines of the project).

These elements underpin the description of a 'successful' project as one that is completed within budget, on time and to the expected standard of quality. For postgraduate research projects, the two elements that usually take priority are time and quality. Your supervisors should have planned a project that is financially feasible, although you will need to clarify whether the costs of your planned tasks are affordable. More importantly, the deadline for your funding is (usually) fixed; therefore, quality will suffer if you run out of time to complete the thesis within the

Table 3.1 Terminology associated with project management

Term	Explanation
Project	A sequence of activities designed to achieve a specific outcome within a defined budget and time limit.
Goals	Describe what is to be achieved.
Objectives	Provide a specific, measurable description of what is to be achieved. In research, objectives correspond to research questions.
Tasks	Describe units of work.
Deliverables	Clearly defined outputs from the project (the product of work).
Schedule	Describes the timing of a list of tasks to be performed.
Milestone	Defines a time point when a series of related tasks are to be completed.
Deadlines	Defines a time point by when deliverables must be produced.
Planning	Development of a detailed scheme to attain an objective.
Project plan	A written description of the work needed to complete the project, including a description of the tasks, organisation and management of the project.

allotted time, or an extension of the deadline is required to deliver the expected standard of quality.

There are five main phases associated with the successful management and execution of a project: initiation, planning, executing tasks, monitoring of progress and completion.

- *Initiation* includes important activities such as a student's selection and application for a project, liaison with a potential supervisor and registration at a university. These topics are discussed in detail by, for example, Cryer (2000: Chapters 2–5), and Phillips and Pugh (1994: Chapters 1, 2 and 9).
- *Planning* typically involves a considerable amount of project definition, during which the scope and objectives of the project are clarified. Once the objectives of the project and the research are clear, one can identify the tasks that must be conducted to achieve these objectives. In the project plan or research proposal, one then defines the variety of tasks, and schedules their timing and duration. As an effective project manager, you need to continuously plan to cope with change and deviations from your original plan.
- *Execution of tasks*, which requires the majority of the time and effort of the project. This is where the traditional research activities are accomplished (see Table 3.2). However, other project activities also

need to be addressed, such as attending training courses, participating in workshops and interacting with other researchers.

- *Monitoring* of project progress ensures that the timing, cost and
quality of the tasks proceeds as planned. In addition to your own
monitoring and controlling practices, your supervisor should provide
important guidance. Formal arrangements may also contribute to
monitoring of progress, e.g. formal project meetings, meetings of your
thesis committee, end-of-year meetings, upgrading from MPhil to
PhD.

- *Completion* of the project involves such activities as production of
a final report (the thesis), the PhD examination, dissemination
of the research findings (publications and presentations), and
acknowledging the contribution of others.

There is a typical sequence to these phases, many of which overlap (see
Figure 3.1). A variety of common practices within PhD projects correspond to these five phases and represent elements of good project
management (see Table 3.2), e.g. the definition of research questions and
hypotheses, the timetabling of various tasks, and reviewing the progress
of the research. Presumably, research students conduct these activities
most of the time. However, it is important that *your conscious recognition
of the interdependence of these activities, and how they assist your progress,
should encourage you to actively undertake and co-ordinate these project
management activities during your PhD project.*

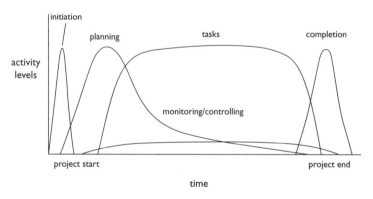

Figure 3.1 Phases of research projects

Table 3.2 Description of activities that typically occur during a PhD project, and how they correspond to project management practices in different phases of a typical PhD project

Project phase	Management activity/issue	Corresponding activity in PhD project
Initiation	Initiation	Project selection, supervisor selection, interviews, registration.
Planning	Definition of objectives and scope	Defining research questions that make an original contribution to knowledge, clearly delimit the boundaries of investigation; define the expected quality (Chapter 1).
	Project plan	Written research proposal/plan; information on scope, conceptual background; justification and description of research methodology (Chapter 1).
	Task list	Details of various tasks and activities
	Scheduling	Indication of the sequence, timing and duration of the research tasks (Chapter 3).
	Deliverables	Data sets, analyses, progress reports, thesis and publications. These must be of appropriate quality.
	Milestones	Completion of literature review, completion of surveys or experiments, feedback from annual meeting of supervisors and thesis committee, first draft of a thesis chapter.
	Management	Identifying the roles and responsibilities of supervisor and student (Chapter 2), meetings, achieving agreement and consensus, identifying skills competencies (Chapter 2), and training needs for research and professional development.
Execution of tasks	Preparatory tasks	Literature review (Chapter 4); details on background, justification and conceptual framework (Chapter 4), training for specialist tasks, defining the research methodology, pilot research projects.
	Main tasks	Training for research and professional development; networking and collaborating; 'doing research': data collection from surveys, interviews or experiments, the storage, analysis and interpretation of data, writing the thesis and publications (Chapters 5 and 6), presenting your results.

Table 3.2 continued

Project phase	Management activity/issue	Corresponding activity in PhD project
Monitoring	Detecting and addressing deviation from the objectives, schedule or quality	Monitoring progress; communicating progress (positive/negative developments and any proposals for change) to supervisors; the supervisor and thesis committee will provide expertise, guidance and feedback (Chapters 2 and 5); upgrading from MPhil to PhD.
Completion	Produce deliverables of required quality and on time Completion	Editing and proofreading of thesis; submission of thesis, undergo *viva*, finalise publications, publicise the research findings (Chapters 5, 6 and 7). Handover of equipment; archiving of data, acknowledging assistance, reflection on lessons learned and contribution of the project to your professional development and future career (Chapters 1 and 7).

The project management approach: an overview

Exercise 3.1 considers a variety of project management issues in the context of your PhD project. Depending on how long you have been doing your PhD, you will be better able to answer some questions than others. The value of this holistic overview is that it demonstrates the project management 'mind-set'.

You need to consider wider issues in the goals and objectives of your PhD project than the research alone: such issues are well represented in Table 3.2. Thus, important project objectives would address not just your research questions but also, for example, attendance at relevant training courses, or a commitment to develop networking relationships with other researchers. It is important to recognise the importance and priority of such activities in your PhD project so that they are given appropriate time and energy.

Exercise 3.1

This important exercise encourages a project management approach to your PhD project. In answer to each question, quickly

continued

write down three to five main points. Your answers will be used for comparison with a later exercise.

Definition of objectives

1 What are the goals of your PhD project?
2 What is the justification for and background to your project?
3 What are the objectives of your project?
4 Are your project objectives SMART*?

Breakdown of work

5 What are the specific accomplishments and deliverables of your project?
6 What are the detailed tasks required to produce the deliverables and achieve each of the objectives?
7 Are some tasks dependent on the completion of other tasks?
8 Estimate the duration of each task.
9 Estimate the costs associated with each task.
10 Which tasks are most important? Why?
11 Which tasks are most time-consuming?
12 Which tasks are most difficult? Why?
13 What are the responsibilities of supervisors or other individuals associated with the project?

Execution of tasks

14 What methodology and methods will be used in the research?
15 What specific skills or resources are required, e.g. statistical analyses, laboratory methods, improved writing skill or computer software?

Risk assessment

16 What factors might threaten the successful completion of tasks?
17 How can you minimise or eliminate such impediments to progress?

18 Why do you think some PhD projects succeed better than others?

19 What can you learn from successful and less successful PhD projects?

Monitoring of progress

20 Define 'progress' in the context of your PhD project.

21 How will you know (rather than relying on intuition) that you are making satisfactory progress?

22 How will you monitor your progress?

23 How will you know that you are on schedule?

24 How will you know that your work is of appropriate quality?

* Specific, Measurable, Attainable, Realistic and Time-bound

There is a significant requirement for PhD students to carefully plan the management and execution of the PhD research, as evident from Exercise 3.1. The next few sections of this chapter are devoted to project planning, with a discussion of the benefits and practical suggestions to assist the planning of your project and the monitoring of progress.

An introduction to project planning

In a number of ways, your planning will ultimately guide the practical implementation of the research and govern the quality of your research findings. The quality of your research is of utmost importance: when your PhD thesis is examined, the examiners will not inspect the financial budget for the project and they will assume that the thesis has been submitted within the relevant time limits; therefore, the examiners will be almost exclusively concerned with the quality of the thesis. Such emphasis on research quality in the PhD examination both explains and justifies the requirement for effective planning.

Why plan?

Many students skimp on the planning stages of the PhD project; therefore, this section highlights the importance of planning. Most importantly, planning supports the quality of your research in a number of ways. Proper planning at the beginning will result in more focused objectives and a clearer understanding of the demands of the project. Such understanding is important to ensure that your decision-making and actions are consistent with the strategic objectives of the project. This is especially important when unforeseen circumstances arise, whether they are threats or opportunities.

The PhD project requires a long-term integration of effort, some of which can be quite complex. Planning will help to clarify and manage such complexity and thereby increase the likelihood of completing the project. Effective planning will help you to break up a large project into a series of more manageable tasks that nevertheless maintain a co-ordination towards the main objectives. Such an approach will also allow you to better identify requirements of the project, e.g. finance, equipment, time, scheduling and research skills.

One important implication is that these planning and management activities take time, as well as considerable intellectual effort and dis-cipline. The prominence of methodological concerns in the PhD examination highlights the thorough planning and forward thinking that need to occur before the practical research tasks begin (Chapters 1 and 7). Such considerations should convince you not to resent the time that is spent on planning and on other project management activities; con-sider such time to be as valid a part of your research project as collecting and analysing information, and reporting your research findings.

Some main advantages of planning are that it does the following:

- Reduces the risk of overlooking something important.
- Helps you to realise when you have run into difficulties.
- Shows you the relationship between your activities.
- Orders your activities so that everything does not happen all at once.
- Indicates whether your objectives are feasible in the time available. If not, something needs to change.
- Helps you to ensure that the required resources are available when you need them.
- Provides discipline and motivation by indicating targets or mile-stones, and thus is good for morale as you pass each milestone. It shows you are getting somewhere! Experience suggests that the best way to successful completion of the project is the successful completion of intermediate stages.

(modified from Wield 2002: 59–60)

The 'activity trap'

Researchers who do not take sufficient time to plan their project risk falling into the 'activity trap'. At the beginning of a research project, it is tempting (and common) to begin doing research as soon as possible. There can be considerable satisfaction in being very busy at such an early stage of a project. However, such short-term satisfaction is both misguided and at the expense of longer-term strategic planning:

> [At the start of their research], researchers may . . . well want to 'get on with it' and not think about apparently obtuse issues of design. Unfortunately, this is a short-sighted view and it is unlikely to produce research that has instantly recognised merit.
>
> (Trafford and Leshem 2002: 46)

The activity trap confuses being busy with achieving progress. Getting caught in the activity trap leads to poor planning and poor integration of effort. After a few months, when the first phase of activity is completed, a researcher is left wondering what to do next. In the absence of clear objectives to inform strategic decision-making, the researcher either stops and does the planning that was originally neglected or, worse still, continues aimlessly on to the next phase of activity. Richard Billows discusses the activity trap further in 'Project planning: the really creative and highly political first step' (http://www.4pm.com/articles/projplan. html).

Your planning will need to incorporate change

It is important to stress that planning is not the same as blueprinting. Blueprinting implies an inflexible schedule with a series of tasks that must be completed, without any deviation from the original schedule. Hopefully, your planning will mean that you will have avoided or anticipated the major problems, even if minor problems will arise. However, no project goes 100 per cent according to plan, and unexpected circumstances may occur that will have a material effect on the decision-making and strategic direction of a project. For example, permission may be denied to access important information or data; key persons may not agree to an interview or may not return questionnaires; bad weather, pests or contaminants may destroy experiments or samples. Alternatively, more positive examples of unpredictable events include an invitation to spend six months doing your research at another laboratory that has state-of-the-art facilities, or an invitation to speak at a conference. As well as these external issues, issues may arise that are internal to the project. For example, unexpected and apparently important research results from your work may suggest a new priority for your research objectives.

The planning of a research project, therefore, must be an *iterative* process that is conducted *throughout* the project. Your planning must balance the need to work effectively toward strategic objectives with the need to occasionally reconsider whether the original objectives are still appropriate. A research project needs to be particularly sensitive to how the unfolding investigation of a research question can reveal opportunities for new investigation and new research questions: 'Research . . . can, in a very general way, be planned, but not blueprinted. One simply does not know what one is going to discover. These discoveries may lead to a complete change of direction' (Berry 1986: 5). Be prepared to adapt your research plan, but recognise why this is necessary, and have good reasons for doing so. In consultation with your supervisors, you will identify what changes are necessary, and assess the impacts of these changes on your project objectives.

Practical implementation of project planning

Lock (1988: 140–1) identifies seven distinct steps in the planning phase of a project that should be undertaken to establish a work programme:

1   Define the objectives.
2   Divide the project into manageable parts.
3   Decide, in detail, what has to be done and in what sequence.
4   Estimate the duration of each separate activity.
5   Use the estimates of the duration of each activity to calculate the estimated project duration, and the relative significance of each activity to timescale objectives.
6   Reconcile the programme with the resources that can be mustered.
7   Assign tasks to individuals by name. This step is more relevant to projects with several individuals on the project team. It is likely that the PhD student will do most of the tasks, but some work may be dependent on others, e.g. feedback and agreement from supervisors, involvement of technical staff or provision of information by individuals in external organisations.

The rest of this section elaborates on some of the main steps in the above framework for planning a project.

Define the objectives

The early months of a PhD programme are crucial in shaping the future direction of the research programme. Some PhD projects begin with very clear objectives and it may be reasonably obvious what experiments are required, at least for the first year of the research programme. Other projects begin with less-defined objectives, and there is a greater onus on the student to clarify them. In the case of research projects, it is crucial that you have clear objectives, which in turn will help to define the research tasks that need to be conducted to achieve the objectives. Your literature review (Chapter 4) and discussions with your supervisor and other researchers will provide important guidance on your selection of research objectives.

Towards achieving clarity in objectives, project managers attempt to formulate SMART objectives, i.e. objectives that are Specific, Measurable, Attainable, Realistic and Time-bound. These SMART characteristics are further explained as follows:

Specific: the objective is well defined and unambiguous.

Measurable: there is a quantitative method for determining if progress toward the objective is being achieved or not.

Agreed upon: the objectives are agreed (with all supervisors, for example).

Realistic: the objective is achievable within the limitations of resources, knowledge and time.

Time-bound: the time required to conduct the tasks is considered and there is a stated deadline for the achievement of the objective.

The SMART approach is particularly useful for the formulation of testable research questions. For example, the following four versions of a research objective differ in how SMART they are:

- To improve the efficiency of solar panels.
- To improve the efficiency of solar panels by 40 per cent within two years.
- To increase the energy conversion ratio of a solar panel of area 1 m^2 by 2 per cent within two years.
- To improve the efficiency of technology for renewable energy.

The requirement to be realistic is particularly relevant to students beginning a PhD, who tend to be over-ambitious when defining the objectives. It is much better to conduct a project of more limited scope to a high standard, than to struggle with a project that involves too much work. Thus, the doctoral project should be *manageable*, and 'not so complex that it does not allow for normal PhD treatment and completion in a reasonable time' (Lawton 1997: 8). The range of activities described in Table 3.2 is considerable, and indicates that the objectives for the PhD degree include more than just research. By properly identifying the range of skills, demands and components of the PhD research degree, you can begin to ensure that you address the issues relevant to both your research needs and professional development, and avoid neglecting important issues that you might otherwise encounter by serendipity or not at all. It is worth remembering that all of the typical doctoral activities listed in Table 3.2 are expected to be completed in three years (or the appropriate registration period for your degree). A classic problem, unfortunately, is that many students too often fail to appreciate the breadth of activities that a doctoral project requires, and often spend too much time collecting excessive amounts of data and too little time on the other aspects, especially the actual writing of the thesis.

It is essential that you meet regularly with your supervisor throughout your PhD, but particularly in the early stages of the project to discuss, clarify and agree the objectives. If appropriate, approach other members of staff in your department who conduct research in a relevant subject area. They will almost certainly have suggestions that could help you and direct you to relevant reading. However, it is courteous to inform your supervisor before speaking to others. When requesting help from researchers (particularly those in external organisations), be professional and courteous. It is best to request quite specific assistance from such researchers – this indicates that you have already invested time and effort in reading and understanding the subject. Again, inform your supervisors who you are approaching. When contacting people at other institutions, be particularly careful to portray a professional image – make sure that you are prepared, that your questions are clear and concise, and that any letters/emails are well presented and free of typing errors. Use institutional email addresses and, if possible, make up a business card with your details on it. Many PhD students have a 'Steering Group' or 'Thesis Committee' that is composed of a few individuals (in addition to the supervisor) whose role is to provide additional guidance and feedback to the research student.

Divide the project into manageable parts and decide, in detail, what has to be done and in what sequence

Taken as a whole, the PhD project is a daunting prospect. It is advisable (and usually necessary) to divide it into smaller, more manageable areas of work. In any case, the splitting of the project into major areas of work facilitates the identification of the associated accomplishments and deliverables (e.g. see Figure 3.2). At this stage, consider the specific deliverables of your project: what tangible output is to be produced from each of your major areas of work so that you know the output has been delivered? For example, a vague aim of 'professional development' does not clearly indicate how this aim is to be achieved; however, the milestone of 'professional development' in Figure 3.2 will be achieved when the student has completed the specified activities that relate to training, publication, presentation and attendance at various meetings of researchers. Similarly, the deliverable from a research experiment may be a specific data set, which can then be analysed, interpreted and reported in the thesis.

One very important function of project planning is to provide an unambiguous and detailed written explanation of the research methodology, which will underpin your research tasks and ultimately determine the validity, reliability, analysis and interpretation of your research (see Chapter 1). For example, before any practical work is conducted, a methodology for quantitative research should clearly indicate to you and your supervisors the approach to be taken to incorporate research design principles such as replication, randomisation, blocking, independence, and experimental control (e.g. see the Statistical Good Practice Guidelines provided by the Statistical Services Centre at The University of Reading at http://www.rdg.ac.uk/ssc/develop/dfid/ booklets.html).

Risk assessment

A variety of limitations may present themselves during the course of a research programme. It is necessary to appreciate what these might be, and to figure out how to progress with your objectives while incorporating the constraints. While it is not exhaustive, the following list indicates some limitations that might arise:

- How difficult is the project? How much time is required to improve existing skills and learn new skills (e.g. project management, sampling methodologies, seminar presentations, data handling and

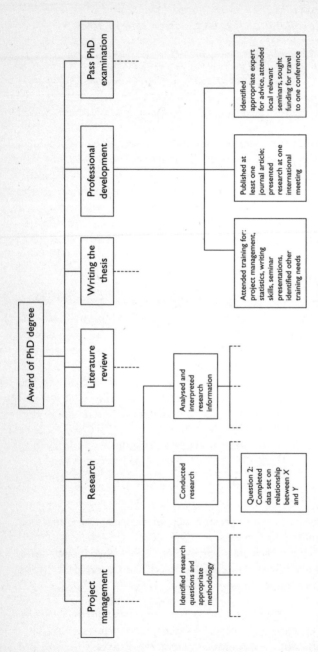

Figure 3.2 Make your PhD project more manageable by identifying the specific accomplishments and deliverables

statistics, computer programing and modelling, chemical analyses, interviewing techniques and questionnaire design)? Where can you get the necessary training?

- Do you need technical or specialist assistance with some of the research methods?
- How much time is required to conduct and complete the project?
- Will permission be required to sample at field sites, conduct interviews or analyse data collected by other researchers?
- Will permission be required from an Ethics Committee for experimentation involving human subjects or live animals? When does the Ethics Committee next meet?

A related and important issue is an assessment of the health and safety risks involved in conducting the work. Such assessment is usually mandatory for laboratory or field work that may involve, for example, use of chemicals, use of equipment with moving parts or visits to remote or dangerous locations. However, health and safety assessments and recommended practices are also associated with, for example, the use of office chairs and computer screens. Most institutions now provide courses on risk assessment and health and safety, and your supervisor will provide you with further guidance; you should immediately inform your supervisor of any health and safety concerns that you have.

In addition to these operational risks that are associated with the implementation of work, there may also be risk associated with the process of discovery that characterises any effort to make an original contribution to knowledge. The most novel, interesting and rewarding research questions are those to which we do not know the answer. Therefore, although we can identify such risk, it is perfectly acceptable. The magnitude of the risk may differ considerably, as the answer to some questions may be guessed quite confidently, whereas the outcome of other questions may be truly difficult to guess (and the magnitude of original contribution to knowledge is correspondingly higher). Many students and supervisors try to spread the risk by undertaking a combination of low-, medium- and high-risk research. Thus, even if the high-risk research does not go well (as sometimes happens, but even these events can be usefully documented in the thesis), there is the low- and medium-risk research to ensure that there is a sufficient original contribution to knowledge.

Box 3.1   Vital risk prevention

Every risk assessment should identify the loss of information as a risk. Note that many funding agencies and research institutions place a clear responsibility on a researcher to have back-up copies of their research and data. To lose research data may be considered a form of academic misconduct.

Most research students are quite dependent on their computer as a storage device for research plans, reference collections, databases, literature reviews, thesis chapters and draft manuscript. However, computer storage is not 100 per cent dependable: hard drives may malfunction for no apparent reason; an office flood or accident may destroy your hard drive; office fires are rare, but rare events do happen; computer viruses can destroy all your work (use an up-to-date virus-checker), and important files can be accidentally deleted.

Store a back-up copy in a separate building – if both are kept in the same building, a fire or flood may destroy both the hard drive and the back-up copy. The back-up copy needs to be regularly updated; otherwise, its use as a back-up rapidly diminishes over time. It is advisable to make a back-up copy of all your electronic files on at least a weekly basis. Floppy disks are not reliable storage devices: zip disks and CDs are much more reliable. Enquire about the possibility of making back-up copies on the local server; this is very convenient for making daily back-ups of regularly used files (*in addition* to your back-up copy that is stored at a separate location).

Keep your record sheets for the duration of the project at least, but many projects have commitments to keep record sheets for much longer. Again, keep paper copies of important information in two separate locations. It is also a good idea to keep paper copies of electronic spreadsheets that contain your raw data.

Planning a time schedule

Full-time PhD studentships are typically for a period of three years, so you have a finite period of time available. Your plan must include a realistic and feasible time schedule, or you risk running out of time, which may result in sub-standard work. Faced with a three-year period of research, new PhD students sometimes wonder how they are going to keep themselves busy for all this time; however, they soon realise that time is a precious resource in doctoral research projects.

Planning your time: the bigger picture

Before discussing in detail the duration of different tasks, it is worth looking at the bigger picture for a few moments. This involves reflecting on the main aims of the PhD as a demonstration of your successful learning to make an original contribution to knowledge and provide evidence of critical evaluation. In support of these aims, therefore, some of the most important elements of planning and implementation will focus on issues such as: reviewing, learning and understanding theory; devising questions that test developments in theory; devising research methods that are appropriate to the research questions; critically evaluating the research findings, and writing the thesis to a doctoral standard. These activities require time, but it can be difficult to predict how *much* time. Less obviously, these activities also require a certain state of mind, one that has the opportunity and composure to engage in critical reflection, consider alternative views, debate pros and cons, weigh up issues and arrive at informed and reasoned judgements. Therefore, in order to have such opportunity and composure, it is incredibly important that you are not so busy that you literally do not have time to think – to do so is to fall into another version of the activity trap.

Where this discussion relates to scheduling of activities is that you should not plan for every available hour to be spent on practical research tasks; indeed, you should leave a substantial amount of your time unscheduled as contingency for inevitable delays and under-estimates of the time required to conduct project activities. Naturally, there will be short periods of days or weeks when you may be exceptionally busy and will be too pressured to engage in reflection – this is quite normal, and these periods represent the implementation of your research plans. However, such bursts of activity are normally interspersed with calmer periods; students who have to work for several months without any time to think need to seriously consider the focus and feasibility of the research objectives and tasks.

Estimating the duration of major tasks

The feasibility of a project will be dependent on a realistic effort to schedule the timing and duration of various tasks. The use of some form of a time budget is advisable to help raise your awareness of the time demands of different components of the whole project, and ensuring that you forecast an appropriate distribution of time among the different tasks. A common approach is to construct a time budget, which lists the tasks and activities appropriate to your project and estimates the amount of *elapsed time* required for each activity (e.g. see Figure 3.3). Obviously, you will be quite uncertain about some estimates, and it may be useful to indicate both the shortest and longest time that you estimate will be required (as in Figure 3.3). You can also ask other PhD students for their

List of major tasks	Smallest estimate of required time	Greatest estimate of required time
Project management		
Project scoping and definition	....	....
Project planning	....	....
Meetings and reporting	....	....
Communications, e.g. email, phone and letter	....	....
Professional development	....	....
The literature review		
Defining the objectives	....	....
Sourcing and reading the literature	....	....
First draft	....	....
Revising and editing	....	....
Investigation 1		
Define research questions	....	....
Conduct sampling	....	....
Process samples	....	....
Record data	....	....
Data input	....	....
Data analysis and interpretation	....	....
Investigation 2 ...	....	....
Investigation 3 ...	....	....
Writing the thesis		
First draft	....	....
Revising and editing	....	....
Incorporate feedback from supervisor	....	....
Proofreading	....	....
Printing the thesis	....	....
Total		

Figure 3.3 A template of a time budget to estimate the amount of time required to conduct some of the major tasks in a doctoral project

opinion on the amount of time that will be required for various elements in your time budget.

The following example illustrates how quite rough calculations in a time budget can quickly indicate the feasibility of a research proposal. Consider a research plan that depends on three major investigations. The first investigation will generate about 950 replicate samples (it may help to think of each sample as a returned questionnaire, or a biological sample that is examined under a microscope, or some unit of work relevant to your research). If each sample takes one hour for the associated sampling and processing, then the sampling of this first investigation will require 950 hours. Assuming a seven-hour working day (excluding breaks) and a five-day week, this is equivalent to about 27 weeks. Using the same assumptions and allowing time for holidays, there are about 35 working weeks per year. Thus, the sampling, and only the sampling, for the first investigation will require more than three-quarters of the year.

However, the calculated 27-week period allows no time for any other activities or events that normally occur in doctoral research, such as project planning, reading, writing, discussing your research with others, responding to emails, reporting on progress, attending training events, illness, entering data to a spreadsheet, analysing the data, part-time teaching, tutoring, and so on. Therefore, assuming that these essential activities will occur, the *elapsed* time for the first investigation is quite certain to exceed one year.

With such information, informed judgements can be made. As one scenario, it may be that this first investigation is intended to be a pilot study; if so, then it is probably far too demanding and is likely to prevent the timely completion of the more important second and third investigations. Alternatively, if the first investigation is to be the most important investigation of the three, then it may continue as planned, but the second and third investigations may need to be reduced in size if the thesis is to be completed within three years. Another alternative scenario is that the time budget for all three investigations indicates a required total time of almost five years, and the investigations cannot be reduced in size without compromising their statistical validity (for example). Then, perhaps only two of the investigations would be conducted, or a decision needs to be taken that the planned series of investigations is not feasible within the allotted timeframe and must be abandoned in favour of a feasible project.

Exercise 3.2

In Exercise 3.1, you listed the tasks and activities associated with your project. At this point, allocate the amount of elapsed time that you estimate would be required by each of the tasks and activities in your project. It is likely that you will be more confident about some of these estimates than others. Table 3.2 and Figure 3.3 may provide a useful guide, but you will need to construct a time budget that reflects the specific requirements of your research project.

Project planning: how to incorporate unpredictability?

Even for experienced researchers, it is difficult to predict how future conditions will affect even those projects with clearly defined objectives. In the case of research projects, there is the added dimension that original research involves a process of discovery that will sometimes proceed as initially planned, but will often provide unexpected outcomes, detect research directions that turn out to be blind alleys, and discover research directions that may be far more promising than the original ones. I have already mentioned the need for research planning to be able to adapt and incorporate the variety of changes that may occur during a research project, but a criticism of traditional project management (see Figure 3.4) is that it is not sufficiently flexible to cope with such unpredictability (see Austin 2002, 'Project management and discovery', available online at <http://nextwave.sciencemag.org/cgi/content/full/2002/09/10/4>). An alternative approach to managing a research project with (to some degree) unpredictable outcomes is to introduce decision-making at various time points. The components of Figure 3.5 provide an example of *adaptive management* that acknowledges and manages the uncertainty associated with original research. The project begins (1) with the usual activities of objective-setting, planning, implementation and monitoring of progress. A decision-making process (2) occurs, during which an informed decision is made whether to continue with the original plan (3), or whether some form of modification is required (4). If change is required, the objective and project management are modified accordingly (5), the project implemented, and the progress evaluated again at another decision-making event (6), and so on. The benefit of adaptive

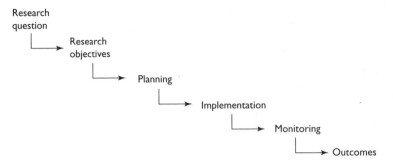

Figure 3.4 Typical stages of a PhD project

management is that it actively manages unpredictability by either confirming the original objectives (when no change is required) or modifying the objectives and planning to take account of a change in circumstances (cf. Figures 3.4 and 3.5). In practice, this method enjoys widespread use in doctoral projects whenever students and supervisors (or Thesis Committees) agree that the current objectives are progressing well, or that the objectives or research practices need to change when progress is unsatisfactory. However, there is rarely an explicit recognition of this facility to adapt the project to cope with change and discovery.

Of course, adaptive management may be neither necessary nor suitable for some projects. For others, however, it provides a more responsive reaction to changed circumstances:

> Adaptive frameworks assume that the future grows hazy rather quickly the farther you look into it. They therefore concentrate efforts on a shorter horizon, after which they assume there will be an abandon-or-continue decision and a revision of plans . . . In some cases adaptive frameworks encourage you to just go ahead and try something rather than devote a lot of time to detailed planning. You may learn more from the experience of trying than you could ever learn by thinking about it in planning.
>
> (Austin 2002)

The latter half of this quote is not a licence for abandoning a strategic approach to research; however, within an overall guiding framework that is informed by your judgement and intuition, this 'give-it-a-try' approach certainly corresponds well with the investigative and exploratory nature of original research.

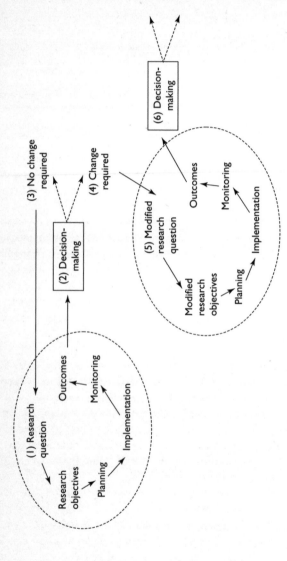

Figure 3.5 Adaptive management includes decision-making to consider changes to research projects

Another perspective on adaptive frameworks is that they may give rise to two types of planning – outline planning and detailed planning. Outline planning gives an overview of the expected main project deliverables and tasks over the full duration of the project (the hazy future), whereas detailed planning provides the level of information that is needed to implement the project within the forthcoming six- , nine- or twelve-month period (the shorter horizon). Most importantly, an outline plan provides you with a 'mental map' of the various activities that occur throughout the PhD programme (such as those in Table 3.2). Such a mental map provides an overview of the integration across various components of the research and the PhD project – this provides a sense of control that is very empowering (and reduces stress associated with uncertainty). As an example of outline planning, Table 3.3 gives an example of an outline research plan that a new PhD student has produced for the first year of their degree, which indicates the main aims for each two-month period over one year (the outline plan for the second and third year would also be produced by the student). As an example of detailed planning, Figure 3.6 demonstrates a schedule of the main elements associated with specific research tasks to be conducted over a six-month period, using weekly periods. Other associated elements of detailed planning would include, for example, a detailed description of the research objectives, the research methods, analytical techniques, and so on. Detailed planning corresponds to the activities within the dashed circles in Figure 3.5.

Note that outline planning is not an excuse for sloppy planning. Outline planning is intended to complement, not substitute for, detailed planning; a reliance on outline planning alone should not be used to justify procrastination on the intellectual challenge that is often associated with detailed planning. You need to begin your project with a commitment to a programme of work for the duration of the project, so that there is a planned 'default' project in the event of a decision *not* to make changes.

For further excellent discussion of research management that facilitates the unpredictability associated with original research, see Austin (2002) and Portny (2002, 'Project management in an uncertain environment', available online at http://nextwave.sciencemag.org/cgi/content/full/2002/ 08/21/3); see also the related articles.

Table 3.3 Example of an outline plan for the first year of a doctoral research project

Tasks	Oct–Dec	Jan–Feb	Mar–Apr	May–June	July–August	Sept–Oct
Meetings with supervisor	Discuss and clarify objectives of project	Discuss literature review and project outline and get feedback on selected research questions	Discuss experimental design and sampling methodology	Inform supervisor of progress of fieldwork	Inform supervisor of progress of fieldwork	Discuss detailed plans for year 2 and outline plan for year 3
Project planning	Clarify objectives of project	Submit project outline to supervisor; prepare project schedule for fieldwork season (Mar–Oct)	Plan experimental design of pilot experiments; refine experimental design and sampling protocols; assess health and safety issues; meet statistician to discuss experimental design; create record sheets and spreadsheet for raw data	Enter raw data from record sheets into spreadsheet; file record sheets	Enter raw data from record sheets into spreadsheet; file record sheets	Preliminary analyses of data; start detailed planning for year 2

Table 3.3 continued

Tasks	Oct–Dec	Jan–Feb	Mar–Apr	May–June	July–August	Sept–Oct
Literature review	Clarify aims, start literature review; visits to library for journal references	First draft of literature review; identify hypotheses				Resume work on literature review (after fieldwork season)
Thesis Committee meeting		First meeting at end of February for feedback on plans		Second meeting in May		Third meeting at end of October
Fieldwork		Organise equipment	Conduct pilot experiments and record data	Main experiments and record data	Main experiments and record data	Finish fieldwork in mid-Oct
Training and other events	Induction course; health and safety; attend conference in mid-December	Present project outline at departmental seminar	Attend 1-day statistics workshop on March 12th	Attend 2-day training course on 'Advanced use of spreadsheets'		Presentation of Year I activities/results at departmental seminar

WEEK

TASK	23	24	25	26	27	28	29	30	31	32	33	34	35	36	37	38	39	40	41	42	43	44	45	46	47
Formal meeting with supervisor		▨													▨				▨					■	
Computing course				▨	▨	▨		▨																	
Statistics course			▨	▨	▨																				
Teaching/tutorials										▨	▨	▨	▨	▨	▨				▨		▨	▨	▨		
Finalise research questions	■	■	■																						
Identify references for lit. review				■	■																				
Writing literature review						■	■																		
Updating literature review																				■					
EXPERIMENT I																									
Planning/finalise methods				▨	▨	■	■																		
Identify materials							▨	▨																	
Pilot experiment									■																
Fieldwork										■	■	■	■	■											
Input data												■	■												
Analyse data														■	■										
Draft of methods & results																■	■								
Prepare mid-year report																					■	■			
Departmental presentation																						■	■		
Meeting of Thesis Committee																							■	■	
Decisions/planning for year 2																									■

■ Intensive activity   ▨ Less intensive/part time activity

Figure 3.6 Schedule of specific research tasks (Gannt chart)

Determine what resources you will need to get the project done

Compile lists of equipment, other resources or IT software that you will need; determine if the equipment is readily available. If not, consider whether there is an alternative that is available, or ask your supervisor whether the equipment can be purchased. Often, there are tedious administrative procedures and delivery delays associated with the purchase of equipment, so beware and plan your purchases well in advance of when you need the equipment. To check whether there is a sufficient budget for the equipment, consumables, analyses, etc. that you need, develop an estimate of the costs of materials, analyses, consumables and equipment as soon as possible. You will need to discuss these estimates and the expected total budget with your supervisor.

During the course of your project, you will have to rely on many people (apart from your supervisor). You may well be asking technicians for equipment, other academic staff for information, or outside organisations for permission or information. It is worth remembering that you need them more than they need you! Just because you plan to do an experiment tomorrow does not mean that other people have time to get you equipment or provide you with information in 24 hours. Early in the project, therefore, explain to such people what you are doing, and that you may need their help. Forward planning at early stages will allow you to make requests for help well in advance – advance notification will usually give your request higher priority when action is required.

Exercise 3.3

This exercise will help you plan the development of your skills, and consider your understanding of important qualities that will underpin your successful management of your research project. You may wish to refer to Box 1.3 and Exercise 1.4.

1   Identify the research skills that you will need to complete your project.
2   What skills will you need to develop/improve your ability as a researcher and a project manager?
3   How do you plan to achieve this development/improvement?

Plan to complete the project

It is important that you plan the completion of your PhD project with as much attention as you plan both the beginning of the project and the execution of the research. To use a travel analogy, it can sometimes appear as if the destination of a PhD programme is the place where you are when you run out of fuel. Do not let this happen. The end of your PhD project (and your funding) is inevitable and you should plan accordingly. A common problem is that students aim to conduct too much research, and leave an inadequate amount of time at the end for analysis and interpretation of the research findings as well as writing, revising and editing the thesis. In such a situation, either the thesis is submitted on time but is of lower quality than expected, or the writing of the thesis takes longer than planned. Other planned activities may also suffer, such as the writing of papers for publication and the presentation of the research findings at meetings and conferences. In the case of a full-time, three-year degree, it is expected that you complete the research and the writing of the thesis in this period – you should not plan for three years of research that is followed by an undetermined period for writing up.

In the final year of your PhD project, the research content of your thesis should be relatively clear. At this stage, consider how much more research you need to do to have 'enough'. Discuss this with your supervisor, and it may help to read other PhD theses to estimate the quantity of work that is typical of a PhD thesis in your research discipline. Then, plan the remainder of the year, making a clear distinction between the completion of ongoing research, the initiation of new research, other activities (training events or conferences) and the completion of the thesis. Such planning activity should help you devise a realistic schedule for completion.

Project monitoring

A number of questions in Exercise 3.1 focused on the monitoring of progress and were aimed at encouraging you to introduce some objectivity into an assessment of your progress.

One advantage (and aim) of project planning is that it facilitates (a) monitoring (detecting deviation from the plan); and (b) controlling of progress (dealing with any detected deviation from the plan). An important point here is that a more objective method of detecting deviation from the plan can be achieved by comparing actual progress with the planned (expected) rate of progress that is necessary to complete within the expected time. At its simplest, such monitoring may involve an inspection of the time schedules (e.g. timetables and Gannt charts in outline and/or detailed plans) to check that deliverables are produced on time, and to identify where deadlines have not been met. Monitoring progress, however, is not just about being punctual; it also needs to consider the quality of the deliverables, and whether the project is within spending limits.

Where deviation from the project plan is detected, the question arises: What to do about it? The answer to this question will depend on each specific situation and whether the source of the deviation relates to time, quality, finance or your professional development; it is difficult to provide general guidance, except to say that your supervisor is available to provide assistance. Towards making as informed a decision as possible, it is advisable to attempt to identify the causes of deviations from the plan, and consider a number of alternative solutions. An excellent discussion of the analyses of problems and decision-making is provided in Kepner and Tregoe (1997).

To assist your monitoring of progress, therefore, it is important that you produce tangible outputs from your planning (e.g. schedules, Gannt charts, time budgets, etc.), and that you do not simply attempt to try and keep all this information in your head. By producing documented records, your research plans will be available for monitoring your progress as well as for future reference and modification – all without the added stress associated with the risk of forgetting crucial information. Such documents are also very useful for communicating your plans to your supervisor and others, and should increase the quality of feedback that you receive on your planned and actual progress.

Responsible conduct in research

The practical implementation of research will require you to conduct sampling and analytical methods that are appropriate to your research discipline. Your supervisor should be an excellent source of guidance on such issues, and most disciplines have numerous relevant books that should be consulted for more detail. More generally, responsible conduct in research is an important aspect of research culture that underpins research practice and quality, but is an issue that often receives inadequate attention.

The conduct and reporting of research projects contribute to the advancement of knowledge and the progress of society. Current researchers trust that previous researchers have conducted and reported their research as accurately and reliably as possible; similarly, future researchers will rely on accurate and reliable reporting by current researchers. This interaction and the dependence among cohorts of researchers were highlighted by Newton's famous quote, 'If I have seen further, it is by standing upon the shoulders of giants.' Therefore, a fundamental requirement and a basic assumption are that researchers should make every effort to honestly produce and disseminate information that is as accurate and reliable as possible.

Despite the importance of responsible conduct in research, these issues are rarely included or discussed in undergraduate or postgraduate programmes. At the same time, the pressures on modern researchers to submit proposals, win research grants and produce publications creates ever more potential for conflict with the values and practices associated with the honest conduct of research projects.

An excellent introduction to such issues is provided by The National Academy of Sciences (NAS) in a document entitled 'On Being a Scientist: responsible conduct in research', available online at http://stills. nap.edu/readingroom/books/obas/. It contains useful discussions, hypothetical situations and dilemmas (and some guidance on how to deal with them) that are very relevant to the ethical and professional issues that young researchers may experience (see Exercise 3.4 for an example). The Danish Committee on Scientific Dishonesty also provides guidance in its 'Guidelines for Good Scientific Practice' (1998), available at http://www.forsk.dk/eng/uvvu/publ/.

Exercise 3.4

Paula, a young assistant professor, and two graduate students have been working on a series of related experiments for the past several years. During that time, the experiments have been written up in various posters, abstracts, and meeting presentations. Now it is time to write up the experiments for publication, but the students and Paula must first make an important decision. They could write a single paper with one first author that would describe the experiments in a comprehensive manner, or they could write a series of shorter, less complete papers so that each student could be a first author.

Paula favours the first option, arguing that a single publication in a more visible journal would better suit all of their purposes. Paula's students, on the other hand, strongly suggest that a series of papers be prepared. They argue that one paper encompassing all the results would be too long and complex and might damage their career opportunities because they would not be able to point to a paper on which they were first authors.

1   If the experiments are part of a series, are Paula and her students justified in not publishing them together?
2   If they decided to publish a single paper, how should the listing of authors be handled?
3   If a single paper is published, how can they emphasise to the review committees and funding agencies their various roles and the importance of the paper?

(reproduced from NAS 1995)

See Appendix 2 for a discussion of this example. Further discussion of other scenarios is available in NAS (1995) at http://stills. nap.edu/readingroom/books/obas/

Breaches of responsible conduct in research can be divided into negligence and misconduct (see NAS 1995), but would not include differences in interpretation or honest mistakes (but when a mistake is detected, it should be communicated to the relevant audience). Negligence occurs when researchers 'provide erroneous information, but have not set out from the beginning with the intent to defraud' (Hammer 1992). Therefore, an important distinction between negligence and misconduct centres on the extent of deception. Negligence typically does not involve premeditated plans to be dishonest. In contrast to an honest mistake, negligent work can result in mistakes that are less much forgivable. For example, the pressures on researchers to win research funding and produce multiple publications can conflict with the time required for designing rigorous experiments, for conscientious working methods and for thorough reflection on the interpretation of research findings. The undue haste and inattention that can arise from such pressures will emerge as preventable errors in the research, which will probably be detected by other researchers.

Misconduct is characterised by premeditated and deliberate attempts to be dishonest. Examples of misconduct include the falsification of data, plagiarism (the presentation of another person's thoughts or words as though they were your own), failure to declare a conflict of interests, the mismanagement of research funds for personal gain and the presentation of other people's work as one's own. The improper allocation of credit and recognition has been a source of serious contention in many disciplines. Breaches of ethical codes of conduct in research are treated very seriously (such as may relate to human and animal experimentation). Other ethical transgressions include: 'cover-ups of misconduct in science; reprisals against whistleblowers; malicious allegations of misconduct in science; and violations of due process in handling complaints of misconduct in science' (NAS 1995).

Such acts of misconduct are extremely serious. They may incur rigorous disciplinary procedures, severely damage a researcher's reputation or result in a loss of employment. Richard Smith (editor of the *British Medical Journal*) provides a fascinating account of different examples of misconduct in biomedical research in 'Research misconduct and biomedical journals' (http://bmj.bmjjournals.com/talks/physics2/index. htm). This is one of several online presentations concerning responsible research practices, available at http://bmj.bmjjournals.com/talks/. An article by Hammer (1992) entitled 'Misconduct in science: do scientists need a professional code of ethics?' discusses such issues further at http://www.chem.vt.edu/chem-ed/ethics/vinny/www_ethx.html.

It may sometimes be extremely difficult to decide whether a particular case is an example of negligence or misconduct; the above categories and examples are intended to illustrate rather than define different points along a spectrum of conduct. Experienced committees usually deliberate on such issues on a case-by-case basis, and such investigations can involve the examination of research notebooks, draft publications, final publications, and examination of research finances. Interviews with relevant individuals may be also conducted to determine a person's motive and degree of premeditation.

Exercise 3.5

Consider the ethical implications of the following scenarios. It may help to consider both the advantages and disadvantages from the viewpoints of different participants in each scenario, e.g. the career of an individual researcher, the research community, funding agencies and the general public:

- Not publishing the findings of a major research project.
- Accepting sponsorship from a multinational company.
- Agreeing to add your name (as co-author) to a paper that you have not read.
- Losing research data because there was no back-up.

If you are in any doubt about an ethical issue, consult your supervisor.

Conclusion

The doctoral project incorporates a wide range of issues that extend beyond the direct activities associated with 'doing research' to issues such as professional development, strategic planning, basic administration, meeting deadlines and maintaining a focus on the quality of the research. Project management is a well-recognised approach to organising such complexity to deliver projects on time, within budget and to an acceptable standard of quality. It is a useful tool that provides principles and strategies that assist your planning, implementation and control of a project in a way that harnesses and disciplines your research imagination into a format that is consistent with the conventions of rigorous research.

There is no single right way to manage a project, just as there is no single way to mismanage one. By presenting some of the more important principles and strategies of project management, I hope to better enable you to use your judgement to select the approaches and strategies that suit your needs as a project manager and thereby help you adopt one of the right ways to manage your specific project.

The project management proverb, 'failing to plan is planning to fail' is particularly apt for PhD students; the emphasis on research quality in the doctoral thesis (see Chapter 1) underlines and demands thorough planning. It is important, however, that you find the right balance between planning and implementation: planning without activity is as fruitless as activity without planning. When implementing your research, be mindful of your duty to conduct your research in a conscientious and thorough manner that accords with the ethics, values and standards of the wider research community.

Recommended reading

Publications

Baker, S. and Baker, K. (2000) *The Complete Idiot's Guide® to Project Management*, 2nd edn, Indianapolis: Alpha Books.

Howard, K. and Sharp, J.A. (1989) *The Management of a Student Research Project*, 2nd edn, Aldershot: Gower.

Kerzner, H. (2003) *Project Management: A Systems Approach to Planning, Scheduling, and Controlling*, 8th edn, New York: Wiley.

Online resources

'Managing Your Research' by the UK GRAD Programme.
http://www.grad.ac.uk/2_2_3.jsp
Introduces a number of online resources to help you manage your research.

Project planning and management.
http://www.mindtools.com/
This website portal links to a number of relevant topics, including project planning and management, stress and time management, creativity and communication.

'Scheduling' by Max Wideman (AEW Services).
http://www.maxwideman.com/issacons3/iac1302/index.htm
An introduction to project scheduling.

'Time management and control' by Max Wideman (AEW Services).
http://www.maxwideman.com/issacons3/iac1301/index.htm

Chapter 4

The literature review

Introduction

Literature reviews are a traditional feature of research and scholarship that all postgraduate students will undertake. Having a clear understanding of your expectations from a literature review will aid your efficient and effective approach to it and make it more interesting for the reader. This chapter clarifies the aims of a literature review, drawing particular attention to the role of critical evaluation in literature reviews. Some guidance is provided on how to conduct a literature review, and some common problems are described.

Literature reviews may be conducted in a number ways by research students, who may interpret and produce a review which is one or more of the following:

- a list of representative literature;
- a search to identify useful information;
- a survey of the knowledge base, disciplines and methodologies;
- a focus on the researcher's gain in knowledge or understanding that is derived from reading the literature;
- a specific focus that supports the research being undertaken e.g. identifying a topic, identifying knowledge gaps, providing a context, deciding on a methodology;
- a written discussion of the literature, drawing on previous investigations.

(modified from Bruce 1994: 221–3)

Note that while most literature reviews will incorporate all the above approaches to some degree, the final three points of this list operate on a higher intellectual level than the first three points. These approaches require a more active and direct interaction with the review material, contribute more to the process of learning, and support reasoned organisation and evaluation. These more demanding characteristics highlight the aim of the literature review to contribute to the scholarship of a subject area, which is expanded on in the following section.

Aims of a literature review

From the perspective of your doctoral thesis and PhD examination, the broader aim of the literature review is to demonstrate your command of your subject area, a professional grasp of knowledge and the ability to evaluate your research and that of others. The literature review allows you to display your 'exercise of independent critical power' that is a requirement of the award of the PhD degree.

A literature review should *critically evaluate* the literature within a particular research discipline with the aim of underpinning and justifying a research question. Unfortunately, many students focus on *summarising* the state of knowledge in their research area; although the role of summary is necessary in a literature review, it is far from sufficient. The review should present an overview of the subject, and its context in the wider research discipline. Thus, the aims, scope, main arguments, underlying concepts, prominent theories and practical applications should be identified and evaluated. The evaluation, or critique, of the reviewed literature is arguably the most important function of the review. Typically, this involves an evaluation of both the quality of the arguments and the evidence that underpin current understanding. Although intellectually demanding, such critical evaluation affords you the opportunity to make a novel contribution to the integration and understanding of your review subject. Note that these higher-level approaches also correspond closely to the issues that must be addressed to demonstrate achievement at doctoral level (Trafford and Leshem 2002; see Chapter 7).

From the above, it should be clear that a literature review should offer much more than a mere summary of a body of knowledge. Good reviews should carry a substantial amount of critical discussion and novel thinking based on the cited work; therefore, simple lists of quotations, data or references do not constitute a good review. The following extract elaborates on the distinction between summary and critical evaluation:

> In notebooks, in newspapers, in handbooks of literature, summaries of one kind or another may be indispensable, and for children in

primary schools it is a useful exercise to retell a story in their own words. But in the criticism or interpretation of literature the writer should be careful to avoid dropping into summary. He [sic] may find it necessary to devote one or two sentences to indicating the subject, or the opening situation, of the work he is discussing; he may cite numerous details to illustrate its qualities. But he should aim to write an orderly discussion supported by evidence, not a summary with occasional comment. Similarly, if the scope of his discussion includes a number of works, he will as a rule do better not to take them up singly in chronological order, but to aim from the beginning at establishing general conclusions.

(Strunk 1918)

In addition to developing, clarifying and creating your conceptual framework, the review should contribute to your search for researchable questions. Very importantly, your undertaking of a literature review should ensure that you do not repeat previously conducted research, in the mistaken belief that it is original. The review should identify knowledge gaps, i.e. areas where understanding is limited or non-existent. Of course, some knowledge gaps may not be easily researchable, and the review may indicate the reasons why. The review may identify existing knowledge gaps that are researchable. Most rewarding, however, is when a review proposes a realistic modification or addition to the conceptual framework of a subject, thereby yielding new knowledge gaps. If feasible, then the PhD research plan will almost certainly be concerned with investigating the validity of a proposed change in the understanding of a subject area.

To summarise, a literature review should not just attempt to illustrate main areas of understanding, but should also point out current areas that are less well understood. Ideally, a review should be able to indicate areas of research that are worthwhile pursuing, but which may have been neglected in the past. Where there are disagreements between studies, some explanation for these disagreements may be provided, if possible. The review should also distinguish between the opinions of the person conducting the review and the opinions from the literature (by referencing the latter). When reading, be alert for opportunities to do the following:

- compare results and conclusions by different authors;
- contrast results that appear to lead to different conclusions;

- reassess results in the light of new information that might not have been available to the original authors.

(Lindsay 1995)

Exercise 4.1

This exercise encourages you to clarify and reflect on the qualities of a good literature review.

1   Select two reviews that are relevant to your subject area. They may be a journal article, a book chapter, an article in a general/popular publication or a literature review from a completed PhD thesis:

   (a) Do you think that they are good examples of a review?
   (b) List the evaluation criteria that you use in making your judgement.
   (c) Are there other evaluation criteria that are more important?

2   For each of the evaluation criteria that you consider to be important, identify specific examples of your chosen reviews that adopt or contravene these criteria.

Conducting the literature review

Have clear objectives

As soon as possible, be very clear on the objectives and scope of the review. When the objectives of a review are not sufficiently specific from the beginning, you can waste a lot of time pursuing literature and ideas that are no longer relevant when you eventually develop more focused objectives. Given the vast amount of information that exists on various subjects, it is necessary to define the scope of the review – this indicates what will be covered in the review, and what will be excluded. You may identify exclusion criteria that relate to language (English language publications only), publication type (peer-reviewed journal articles only) or content. For an example of the latter, consider the following title 'The relationship between socio-economic status and attitudes to education'. A definition of the scope of such a review may consider a number of issues, which include the following: will the review focus on a continent, country or a region? Are you interested in the attitudes of a particular social group? Will the review consider attitudes to primary, secondary or third-level education? If the review focuses on attitudes to third-level education, will it consider undergraduate studies, postgraduate studies or adult education programmes?

You should discuss the objectives and scope of the review with your supervisor, as their experience and insight will be particularly helpful. By precisely describing the scope of your review at an early stage, you will make much quicker progress and save a lot of time and effort that might have been wasted on irrelevant leads. Of course, the objectives, scope and any exclusion criteria should be clearly communicated to the reader. For example, note how the restrictions in the following extract (from a review of an aspect of environmental policy) clearly explain the specific concern of the review:

> First, we briefly describe the differences in design and implementation of agri-environment programmes between countries in Europe. Subsequently we review the effectiveness of agri-environment schemes by surveying all available literature, with the aim of integrating the findings of various studies to produce recommendations for improvement. We have restricted ourselves to the effects of schemes on biodiversity. We only consider schemes implemented until 2000, as the new modified programmes are too recent for proper evaluation. We do not consider set-aside schemes [justification provided] . . . and we do not consider the effects of organic farming [justification provided] . . .
>
> (Kleijn and Sutherland 2003: 949)

Relationship diagrams

Relationship diagrams (e.g. spider diagrams, cluster diagrams, mind maps and flow diagrams) are a very useful and effective way of organising and identifying links between concepts, topics and variables; they are also useful in helping you to maintain an overview of the different components of a complex topic. Relationship diagrams are important because 'they can summarise complex situations, allowing you to appreciate the complexity while seeing the individual components and the connections between those components' (Northedge et al. 1997: 71). They convey information that would be difficult to achieve in a written passage alone, and are excellent for presenting and comparing explanatory frameworks and conceptual models. Used appropriately, such illustrations may significantly advance your 'design, conduct, analysis and presentation of . . . research in a way that consciously achieves and demonstrates doctoral qualities' (ibid.; see Chapter 1).

Relationship diagrams are an extremely useful tool to help clarify and structure thoughts and ideas at various stages of a study or project. Importantly, the construction of a relationship diagram does not just *reflect* your current understanding of a research subject; the construction of a relationship diagram can *actively promote* your understanding and give rise to new insights.

As an example, I have used a relationship diagram to present the components of a successful literature review (see Figure 4.1). I used this particular diagram when preparing to write this chapter and found it extremely useful in clarifying my own thoughts and planning the presentation of the components that typically constitute a good literature review. Figure 4.1 offers a visual summary of the more important points of this chapter; therefore, it reinforces the message from the text. It identifies three clusters of activities and aims of the literature review, the 'Literature search', the 'Conceptual framework', and the 'Review of evidence'. Note that I have structured the diagram so that, in general, the incidence of the higher-level components of the literature review increases from left to right.

Exercise 4.2

This exercise encourages you to use relationship diagrams to structure and evaluate the conceptual development of your research.

1   Figures 4.2 and 4.3 present information on the nitrogen cycle in the form of two versions of a flow diagram. Compare and contrast the two versions of the flow diagram of the nitrogen cycle in terms of differences in how they convey meaning and understanding.
2   As you read research theses and papers, identify examples that have used relationships diagrams to better convey understanding.
3   Draw a relationship diagram that is relevant to your research.

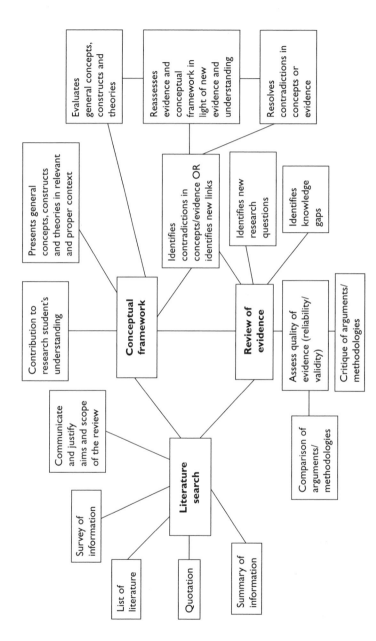

Figure 4.1 Relationship diagram to represent the aims of a literature review

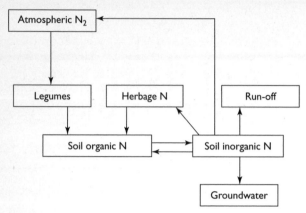

Figure 4.2 Flow diagram of the nitrogen cycle (simple form)

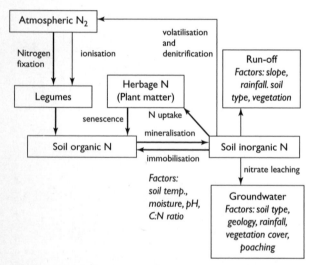

Figure 4.3 Flow diagram of the nitrogen cycle (complex form)

For the purposes of demonstrating the value of relationship diagrams, the subject matter of Figures 4.2 and 4.3 is irrelevant; what is important is the difference in the level of understanding that is communicated. Both diagrams can be used to quickly and succinctly convey information and complex connections between different components, in a way that would be difficult to achieve through a written description alone. Figure 4.2 only indicates patterns and omits the processes; however, Figure 4.3 provides a semi-quantitative representation (that is achieved by changing the width of arrows to indicate the relative importance of different process, and by indicating factors that affect process rates). Comparing these two examples, there is a clear improvement in the number of the components that are demonstrated, how they interact, and the nature of the interactions. Overall, there is a progression in the demonstration and communication of understanding about the subject matter.

Record-keeping

Over the duration of your PhD, you will manage a significant amount of information, part of which is your collection of references. To avoid the frustration of not being able to locate or properly cite an important quote or reference, be meticulous in taking notes, keeping records, constructing bibliographies and referencing.

It is crucial to have an efficient and effective system for cataloguing your references and notes, and for cross-referencing this catalogue to the filed copy. Consider how your collection of journal articles and other references will expand; the investment of some time to develop a systematic ordering and up-to-date database of your references will be well worth the effort. Talk to other doctoral students or your supervisor about the referencing and filing systems that they use.

There are very useful software packages (e.g. Reference Manager, ProCite or EndNote) that can download references from electronic databases, store details of your references, facilitate the construction of a bibliography and implement the required formatting. Given that formatting can differ across so many journals, this can save much more time at publication stage than the time required for the initial typing of the reference details. Most universities provide training in the use of such software.

Critical evaluation

The ability to use your judgement and critical abilities is part of your development and training as a scholar (Chapter 1). One of the fundamental activities of a thorough literature review is the critical evaluation of research articles, which may seem as much an art as a science. Nevertheless, there are a number of criteria or guidelines that may help you, some of which are presented here.

During the literature review, you will undertake several levels of evaluation of articles. Evaluations may vary from a brief inspection to assess the relevance of an article to an in-depth critical evaluation that focuses on the validity and reliability of the research methodology and conclusions. There are a huge number of published articles available across many disciplines, and one important aim is to identify articles of relevance, while quickly dismissing irrelevant articles. The initial inspection of a research article typically encompasses the title and abstract and the nature of the article. The title of an article is the first indicator of its potential relevance to the aim of your literature review. If the title looks promising, then a quick read of the abstract is worthwhile and should help to further confirm whether the article is relevant or not. Another very important factor is the nature of the article. For example, is it published as a personal website, a professional newsletter, an industry-sponsored report, a government report, conference proceedings, a book or book chapter, or a peer-reviewed journal article? These types of publication tend to vary in their level of reliability and credibility. For this reason, the most commonly used type of publication in a review is the peer-reviewed journal article.

Because they are peer-reviewed, journal articles tend to be more authoritative and credible than most other types of publication. However, you need to be careful not to defer to the perceived authority of the journal, which will result in an uncritical evaluation. Even peer-reviewed journals vary in terms of their quality. For example, leading international journals tend to have more demanding standards than smaller national journals. Even then, referees may not detect some flaws in a manuscript. Thus, it should be apparent that even for published, peer-reviewed journal articles you need to conduct a thorough critical evaluation – you are responsible for failing to detect inaccuracies in papers that you review.

How is the evaluation, or critique, of the reviewed literature conducted? Here, I suggest a number of criteria for critically evaluating a research paper. Several of these criteria overlap with the criteria used to assess the quality of manuscripts that are submitted to a journal (see Chapter 6). These criteria are by no means exhaustive, but may serve as a useful guide:

Contribution to your review:

- Is the paper interesting and important? If so, why?
- Is the main argument of the paper relevant to the scope of your review?

- Is there a small section of the paper that is relevant to your review?
- Does the paper agree or disagree with the main argument of your review?
- Does the paper include a comment, idea or speculation that is of interest, and may be worthy of elaboration from the perspective of your review?
- What is the contribution of the paper to the wider research discipline, e.g. advances in theory, concepts or methodology?
- What more specific contribution does the paper make, e.g. identification of causal factors or provision of new data?
- Does the paper conflict with findings by other researchers in the discipline? If so, why?
- How has the research in the paper evolved from previous research?

Research quality of the paper:

- Are the objectives/hypotheses clearly stated?
- Is the justification for the research logically developed and clearly presented?
- Is the research put in the context of the research field as a whole?
- Can you identify how the research fits into, or makes a contribution to, a theoretical/conceptual framework?
- Is the methodology clearly stated and appropriate to the objectives?
- Could the methodology have been improved? How?
- Is the statistical treatment adequate and are the data correctly presented and interpreted?
- Are the conclusions justified by the research findings?
- Are there alternative explanations that could account for the findings, and which have been overlooked by the author?
- Is the paper sufficiently rigorous, accurate and correct?
- Has conflicting evidence been overlooked or ignored?
- Does it give sufficient attention to the literature? Are key references included and are the references up to date?
- Are the limitations of the study identified and discussed?
- Can you identify additional limitations?

Examples of critical evaluation

The following two (fictional) passages highlight the difference between summary and critical evaluation:

Version 1: summary
Smith *et al.* (1997) found no differences in water quality between rural and urban areas, whereas Moore and Park (1998) found significant differences. A survey of water quality among ten different council areas found that water samples in three of ten council areas were consistently in breach of recommended levels over a one-year period (Townsend 2003).

Version 2: critical evaluation
Smith *et al.* (1997) found no differences in water quality, whereas Moore and Park (1998) found significant differences. However, the findings of these two studies are not directly comparable because the first study analysed tap-water samples from urban areas, and the second study analysed groundwater samples from rural areas. A frequently cited survey of water quality among ten different council areas found that water samples in three of the council areas were consistently in breach of recommended levels over a one-year period (Townsend 2003). However, the interpretation of comparisons across the ten areas is unreliable as it is confounded by a number of factors. First, the sampling effort differed across council areas, as the number of replicates from each council area ranged from 45 to 150. Second, the type of analysis different among council areas, as some of the council areas only analysed bacterial content, and others only analysed nitrate levels. Third, slightly different analytical methods were used by each of the councils, although the effects of this difference should be negligible.

Comparing the two versions, it is obvious that version 2 conveys a much deeper methodological insight and provides tangible evidence of critical evaluation, not just summary. As another example of critical evaluation, the following extract discusses academic writing by students, and the different and sometimes conflicting advice provided by experts:

> Many other writers have offered various suggestions concerning writing style . . . Although most suggestions seem reasonable, not all are suited to the conceptual article (or thesis). For example, I disagree with several of Dorn's (1985) imperatives: He said 'Write as you speak' (p. 513). Oral communication does not require the precision of written communication because the speaker receives constant verbal and nonverbal feedback from

listeners. Thus do not write as you speak; write with exquisite and exact finesse.

(Salamone 1993: 76)

Whilst acknowledging Salamone's point, I would think that most students would find the advice that he gives – 'write with exquisite and exact finesse' – somewhat alarming.

(Hartley 1997: 97)

The above passage has Salamone critically evaluating Dorn's advice, followed by Hartley's critical evaluation of Salamone's advice. Note how both Salamone and Hartley accept some points before they add their own clarification and interpretation: it is obvious that neither author has blindly accepted the findings of other researchers. Note also how both authors make their criticisms; their point is clearly made, but is neither personal nor aggressive.

For high-level examples of critical evaluation in your specific discipline, it is well worth inspecting the sections of relevant journals that are devoted to proposing, discussing and sometimes rebutting new concepts and theories. Such sections are often categorised as 'Forum', 'Discussion' or 'Comment'. It can be especially useful to look at past issues of a journal to see the emerging discussion, counter-discussion and synthesis of ideas that are now well established in your discipline.

Structuring your review

Your review should be structured to ensure a coherent and logical presentation. A clear organisation of the review material on central themes will greatly help the reader and demonstrate your mastery of the topic. As you prepare your review, be aware of prominent themes around which the review would be structured. Early identification of such themes allows you to prioritise the relevance of articles. Such themes could include, for example:

- a chronological account of the research subject;
- organisation of material about each of the main conclusions of the review;
- methodological developments;
- developments in theory and conceptual understanding;
- the application of research findings.

Revising the literature review

As a written document, the literature review will involve all the conventions and practices associated with writing (see Chapter 5). However, the revision of the literature review is worth further elaboration. For most students, a version of the literature review is produced at an early stage. For example, a literature review is usually required for an assessment at the end of year one, or for upgrading. However, as you prepare the final version of the thesis, there will almost certainly be a need to revisit and update the literature review written that was written in early stages, for a number of reasons.

It is likely that you will have different aims when reviewing the literature at different stages of your research, and your review will need to be updated to take account of these different aims and approaches. Potter (2002: 120) also discusses this:

> Your purposes of reviewing literature will change as you progress through your research . . . For example, you may be more interested in understanding the results of a piece of work in the early stages of your research, of the research method used once you start thinking about your own data gathering and perhaps why there are differences between your results and those in the literature when your data are gathered in.

At the later stages of your research, you will have an improved understanding of your subject discipline compared to when you first started. Therefore, it is almost inevitable that sections of your review will have to be modified or rewritten to reflect your improvement in understanding as you progress through your project. Approaching the end of your research project, for example, you will appreciate better the strengths or flaws of important papers in your subject; you will have an improved understanding of the theoretical framework that underpins your subject and how this provides a unifying relationship across different research papers; or you will be able to identify new knowledge gaps and new testable predictions.

An important issue for such revision is to consider the relationship between the existing literature and your own research findings. Obviously, this revision will occur late in the doctoral programme, after your research has been analysed and interpreted. Your final revision of the literature review may need to incorporate new advances and publications of significance, and consider how these relate to existing research (including your own). However, you have to balance the need to keep the review up to date with the need to finish the review and submit your thesis – you will not be penalised for failing to refer to an article that was published soon before the thesis was submitted.

Common problems of literature reviews

- The objectives and scope of the review are not well defined. This results in a more superficial 'broad-and-shallow' approach, rather than the more focused and desirable 'narrow-and-deep' approach.
- There is too much emphasis on summary, and insufficient attempts to either critically evaluate the research material, or provide an overview/synthesis. Remember, your own understanding and evaluation should be evident throughout.
- Important conceptual developments are either not referred to or they are explained incorrectly.
- There is limited scope in reading material, with over-reliance on a limited range (and/or quality) of references.
- Older seminal papers and recent important research are not referred to.
- There is an over-reliance on websites and general textbooks (although this is less common in postgraduate research). In increasing order of priority, reviews should focus on academic textbooks, journal review articles and original journal articles.
- There are numerous, obvious mistakes that indicate inadequate proofreading. For example, typographical errors, poor grammar, repeated sentences or paragraphs that have been 'pasted' more than once; references in the text are absent from the bibliography, and vice versa.

Recommended reading

Publications

Chambers, E. and Northedge, A. (1997) *The Arts Good Study Guide*, Milton Keynes: Open University Press.
This book discusses how to get the most out of reading, analysing and evaluating text, and how to improve your writing. Provides lots of case studies and examples.

Hart, C. (1999) *Doing a Literature Review: Releasing the Social Science Research Imagination*, London: Sage.

Murray, R. (2002) *How to Write a Thesis*, Maidenhead: Open University Press.

Online resources

Trent Focus provides a variety of resources for researchers.
http://www.trentfocus.org.uk/
In the 'Resources' section, see 'Carrying out a literature review', 'Managing references', 'Critical evaluation of research' and many other useful guides.

Teaching And Learning at the Environment-Science-Society Interface (TALESSI). http://www.gre.ac.uk/~bj61/talessi/
Go to: Teaching and Learning Resources (TLRs)
Go to: Index of TLRs and authors
See: 1. Bibliographic citation for authoritative academic writing
See: 3. Evaluating the credibility of knowledge claims
See: 32.Virtual climate change: critical evaluation of internet sources.

'PhD: first thoughts to finished writing' by Katherine Samuelowicz, Lesley Chase, and Mandy Symons, Learning Assistance Unit, University of Queensland, Australia.
http://www.tedi.uq.edu.au/phdwriting/

'How to write a PhD thesis' by Joe Wolfe, The University of New South Wales.
http://www.phys.unsw.edu.au/~jw/thesis.html

Chapter 5

Writing the thesis

Introduction

Effective writing is an essential research skill and requires an ability to express your thoughts with clarity, conciseness and some style. PhD students usually have a degree of proficiency at writing, but, unfortunately, there are often implicit assumptions that they are accomplished writers who are automatically able to complete a thesis of about 60,000–80,000 words. The PhD thesis is likely to be the single largest writing activity that research students have undertaken, and larger than most people will ever undertake. Yet, research students rarely think of themselves as *writers*, and there is not always much support to help students develop their writing abilities.

The PhD thesis incorporates issues of research content, structure and style:

- *Research content* is concerned with such issues as originality, the conceptual framework, methodology, achievement of the objectives, and correct analyses and interpretations.
- *Structure* involves appropriate location of different sections of the thesis, logical sequencing of ideas, as well as presentation and formatting of the thesis to the required standard.
- *Style* is a matter of writing with conciseness and clarity, and carefully using the rules of grammar.

(modified from Peat *et al.* 2002: 8–9)

The writing process must address all issues of content, structure and style. A major focus of this chapter is the importance of a well-structured thesis in aiding the PhD examination, along with a description of some of the many activities that contribute to the writing process. I discuss the importance of writing as an aid to developing understanding, and the need for planning and revising of written text. I provide an overview of the thesis as a document that makes a determining contribution to examination and assessment for the PhD degree and the necessity for the thesis to meet the examiners' expectations. Some of these expectations are elaborated on in the section on the presentation, structure and referencing in the thesis.

A detailed discussion about academic writing is beyond the scope of this book, but there are references to some of the many other books and online resources that provide detailed information on writing, complete with writing strategies, case studies and examples of good and poor practice.

The process of writing: an overview

This section discusses some of the main functions and activities associated with writing. It deals with broader issues such as how the act of writing can be instrumental in improving understanding, and a description of important activities such as planning, drafting, revision and feedback. The section concludes with a short discussion about the completion stage of the thesis.

Writing cultivates understanding

Writing is important to develop and clarify your understanding. This may seem strange, as many people believe that their thoughts and ideas need to be fully formed *before* they begin to write. However, this is not always the case: when we write, and *as we write*, we often develop our understanding of a topic:

> [W]riting about more abstract topics is generally difficult, especially if we do not fully understand the ideas we are writing about. . . . [T]he very process of struggling to write about ideas is often clarifying and can promote deeper comprehension.
>
> (Veroff 2001: 203)

> If it is the case that writing leads to discovery, and not, as is generally supposed, that discoveries merely need to be put into writing, this may in part account for the experience of writing the thesis as the most difficult part of the work.
>
> (Phillips and Pugh 1994: 65)

Obviously you don't formulate what you're going to say completely until you come to write it down . . . it was only when I was writing it that I realized that in one section my interpretation was completely wrong. The point I was trying to make just wouldn't embody itself verbally, so I thought it out again and rewrote the whole section.

(research student, quoted in Phillips and Pugh 1994: 67)

Clearly, then, writing achieves more than a careful and accurate record of what you understand *before* you write: writing improves and transforms your understanding *while* you write. It is the struggle to express your thoughts in words that will force you to consider your selection of the most appropriate words, to best describe meanings and to create logical connections between sentences and meanings. This struggle represents a 'no pain, no gain' principle for writers! However, the gain is improved understanding – a fundamental goal of your doctoral research.

If you accept that writing improves understanding, a number of implications follow. First, do not wait to be 'inspired' before you begin to write. A common experience of many PhD students (and many other researchers) is that they often only become inspired *while* they write, in the moments of writing when they struggle to clarify and express themselves. Second, you should start writing from early on in your PhD programme. If writing is an active tool in the clarification and development of your understanding, then it contributes to high quality research. Thus, do not simply relegate the writing of your thesis to the last six months of your programme – otherwise, you will miss out on the full benefit of writing for understanding. These sentiments are implicit in a statement by Murray and Lowe (1995: 103): 'Writing . . . is often seen as the final stage of the PhD process – writing up – rather than as a developmental activity which can be used through the whole research process.' A third implication is that you need to write regularly. Regular writing greatly helps research students to improve their confidence, quality of writing and understanding of their subject. Fourth, you must schedule time for writing (and for learning about writing).

Box 5.1 Characteristic strategies of productive writers

Most productive writers:

- Make a rough plan (which they don't necessarily stick to).

- Complete sections one at a time. (However, they do not necessarily do them in order.)
- Use a word-processor.
- Find quiet conditions in which to write and, if possible, write in the same place (or places).
- Set goals and targets for themselves to achieve.
- Write frequently – doing small sections at a time – rather than writing in long 'binge sessions'.
- Get colleagues and friends to comment on early drafts.
- Often collaborate with long-standing colleagues and trusted friends.

(Hartley 1997: 101)

Planning, drafting, revision and feedback

Planning

A common approach to the planning of writing is to draft major section headings, followed by sub-section headings and then a few notes on the content of each paragraph in the subsections. At this stage, an outline of the chapter (for example) will begin to emerge, and you can start to consider the sequence of major sections. As you refine the logical structure of the chapter, you will become more engaged with the material and decisive about the relevant theme, which becomes a basis for deciding on the inclusion or exclusion of content. The first draft of the chapter then becomes a matter of expressing the main messages of each of the relevant paragraphs.

'The beauty of outlines' by Liane Reif-Lehrer (available at http://nextwave.sciencemag.org/cgi/content/full/2000/06/07/2) provides further excellent discussion, and the related articles are also very useful. The use of relationship diagrams is also a useful tool to assist with planning (see Chapter 4).

Throughout your doctoral research you will be engaged in critical evaluation of others' work; as well as gaining new knowledge, you will also gain new insights and ideas. These are the insights and ideas that will demonstrate your mastery of the topic and original contribution to knowledge – and will form the basis for a lot of written text. Therefore, keep a written record of them in a research journal or a folder. The very act of writing them down will help to develop them further and you will be creating a store of writing that can contribute to your thesis.

Drafting

One reason why research students (and others) feel daunted by writing is the pressure to get a piece of work to a high standard at the first attempt. Permitting yourself to produce draft versions of lower quality is very important in reducing this pressure:

> Early stages, early writings and early drafts will surely lack the quality we expect in the final polished product. Writing that is sketchy, incomplete, tentative and downright wrong is an inevitable part of the research and learning processes . . . While we know that we are not expected to produce high-quality writing – and thinking – in our first, or 'rough' drafts, we have internalised the expectation of high quality writing. This can present writers with a conflict. It can stop them writing anything.
>
> (Murray 2002: 6, 24)

Most writers rely on the iterative process of drafting, rewriting and revision. The first draft of a document, no matter how rough, is valued for generating text and providing (or suggesting) an outline of the content. By forcing the writer to grapple with the issues, first drafts help improve one's understanding of the topic and help a writer to identify issues and text that are not yet contained in the text, but should be. Most importantly, such drafts create a document that can be revised and improved. The message is simple: get the first draft written.

In recognition of the importance (and difficulty) of producing a first draft, many educational researchers and providers of writing courses stress the role of freewriting (e.g. Elbow 1998; Murray 2002). Freewriting advocates the generation of text that expresses your feelings and position on a topic; it is not concerned with accuracy, editing, grammar, audience, style, or coherence because such concerns can inhibit your writing. The method of freewriting is to generate text through non-stop writing for a short period of time (e.g. 10 to 15 minutes); however, the value of this method is its insistence on turning off the 'internal editor':

> Think of the difference between speaking and writing. Writing has the advantage of permitting more editing. But that's its down-fall too. Almost everybody interposes a massive and complicated series of editings between the time words start to be born into consciousness and when they finally come off the end of the pencil or typewriter onto the page . . . But the opportunity to get [words] right

is a terrible burden: you can work for two hours trying to get a paragraph 'right' and discover it's not right at all. And then give up . . .

Editing, *in itself*, is not the problem. Editing is usually necessary if we want to end up with something satisfactory. The problem is that editing goes on *at the same time* as producing.

(Elbow 1998: 4–5)

Guilford (1996, www.powa.org) points out that novice writers 'are too careful and self-critical at the start of a project' whereas more experienced writers 'write quickly, accepting chance discoveries, trusting hunches and gut-feelings, willingly making mistakes'. Again, Guilford's comments highlight the benefits of separating the processes of producing text and editing it. Therefore, freewriting is a useful strategy that addresses your needs as a writer to generate text; it allows writing that is intuitive, creative and exploratory, and allows you to think while you write without distraction from your internal editor. Freewriting is *not* concerned with the accuracy, clarity and purpose that we associate with improved drafts, and is not concerned with the needs of the audience. Such issues are the business of revision and editing. In my experience, I have produced my worst writing while freewriting, but it was relatively easy to improve this subsequently; interestingly, and more importantly, I have also produced my best writing and insights while freewriting.

Freewriting is not a panacea for all writing, and it may be more appropriate to think of it as one of several writing practices, some of which may be more suited than others to a particular situation. For example, when you are writing about more familiar topics, then you may have a clear outline and structure in mind that make it relatively easy to write. However, the original and demanding nature of doctoral research makes it likely that the latter situation will arise on many occasions and you should consider using freewriting as one of your main tools for quickly generating early drafts. Alternatively, freewriting can be very useful when you are struggling to express a new idea, or finding it difficult to write anything at all – at the very least, be willing to try freewriting then.

Revising and editing

Written work needs to be revised on multiple occasions. This is inevitable when you accept (correctly) that a piece of writing cannot be perfect at the first attempt. In this section, I highlight some of the different practices that contribute to the revision and editing of a text.

Experienced writers employ different revision practices from novices. Compared to novice writers, experts address more global problems with structure, are better at detecting problems, and are better able to address these problems (Fitzgerald 1987: 490, in Hartley 1997: 102). Similar differences in revision practices are also evident in the following:

> [E]ach time you revise, you find new potential in the evolving text. Too often, inexperienced writers don't see this potential. They are too careful and self-critical at the start of a project and too easily satisfied toward the end. Having agonized through a first draft, they quickly check for grammar and mechanics and consider themselves done.
>
> More experienced writers usually do just the reverse. Early on, they work at discovering what to say, getting their ideas out onto disk or paper. They write quickly, accepting chance discoveries, trusting hunches and gut-feelings, willingly making mistakes. Gradually, though, they feel a need to look back over their work, to ask whether it makes sense, how their readers will respond. Thus begins the process of revision. Spotting grammatical and mechanical problems is only a minor concern here. Much more important is the need to see the big picture, the overall effect.
>
> (Guilford 1996)

Identifying some of these differences in editorial practice between novice and expert writers also helps to illustrate several different types of editing. The editing process can address issues in the text across different levels, much like the use of a zoom lens: at low magnification, editing may concern chapters, sections and paragraphs; at high magnification, editing may involve the grammar of individual sentences. Here I describe some of the variety of revision practices.

For novice writers, such as most PhD students, there is a wide variety of revision practices to be conducted. For simplicity, I distinguish here between revision of the research content and editing. First, revision of the research content involves a critical evaluation of the conceptual framework presented in the thesis, and an effective communication of the research quality and doctoral worth of the thesis (see 'Expectations of the examiners as examiners', on p. 120). For example, this revision of your own work allows you to improve your understanding of the material, and lets you 'find new potential in the evolving text' (Guilford 1996).

Second, editing in the more traditional sense involves issues such as structure, grammar, punctuation, and spelling:

- *Global structure*: concerned with improving the structure and logical sequence of the document, typically involving decisions on sequence of chapters, sections and paragraphs. Identifies linkage between relevant sections.
- *Layout and presentation*: improved by use of typographical techniques, forecasting, signalling and signposting.
- *Formatting*: checking references, compliance with university guidelines.
- *Clarity of meaning*: such as word selection, sentence structure and removing ambiguity.
- *Style*: achieving accuracy, clarity and conciseness.
- *Grammar, punctuation, spelling, typographical errors.*
- *Other issues*: e.g. mathematical or scientific notations; presentation of figures, tables and their legends; presentation of statistical results; accuracy of calculations.

The aim of this list is not to provide an exhaustive description of editing practices, but to heighten your awareness of their variety. Importantly, many different skills need to be implemented *all at once* when we review text, if the text is to be edited effectively. Given this multitude of critical assessments of text, perhaps it is not surprising that novice writers do not always engage the full repertoire of editing practices – perhaps they are not even aware of this variety? Unless novice writers have learned otherwise, it is understandable (although not excusable) that they 'quickly check for grammar and mechanics and consider themselves done' (Guilford 1996). Until you become more experienced and confident in your editing skills, one way to ensure that you engage the full repertoire of revision and editing practices is to review the text and focus on one editing skill at a time. Therefore, at the first reading you review the research content; at the second, the global structure; at the third, the layout and presentation; and so on. This approach has the added advantage of deciding at an early stage what material needs to be excluded, which saves time that might otherwise have been wasted on fine-scale editing of material destined not to appear in the final thesis.

Global structure

One of the above editing issues, global structure, is worth discussing further. In recent years, the DVD version of many films provides an option to listen to commentary from the director. Such commentary typically provides a rare insight into the tension between the creative process and the need for discipline in editing the global structure of the film (see also Chapter 3). It is fascinating to hear directors explaining their decision-making both when including certain scenes, and removing others from the final version. The agonising of directors is palpable when they decide to cut certain scenes (that were expensive and time-consuming to produce) because they are not relevant to the storyline, are too long, are distracting, or because they slow down the pace of the film too much. Sometimes, such decisions can involve major changes in storyline.

Similarly, you are the director of your thesis. You must make decisions such as what to include and exclude in your thesis, in what order the chapters should appear, and the outline and sequence of sections in each chapter. When evaluating your text, aim to identify whether the existing sequence and content of sections are best structured to maximise the reader's understanding. It is likely that not all of your research will appear in the thesis, and hard decisions sometimes need to be taken: some sections may need further explanation or elaboration while others may need to be deleted. For example, it may not be appropriate to include the detail of some pilot experiments, especially if such experiments had methodological flaws that were detected and removed in subsequent, improved experiments. It may be sufficient to mention that the methodology was improved after conducting pilot experiments (students attending a *viva* should be prepared to expand on the role of the pilot experiments as a learning experience). Some students do not include some perfectly good research theme in their thesis because it is not consistent with the rest of the thesis – it does not support the storyline of the thesis (such research may be published in a journal at a later stage). Of course, the omission of careful research just because it does not provide data that support your argument is unethical – and may be an important oversight: 'if experienced observers, taking all possible precautions, found themselves confronting an anomaly for which they could not account, they were probably "on the verge of some important discovery"' (Keay 2000: 121). In any event, such decisions will be situation-specific and your supervisor will provide guidance.

In practice, revision and editing tend to be most effective when you put a document aside for some time (perhaps a few days) before re-reading it. This 'detachment' from your writing will help you to be more critical of it. Rather than working from the computer screen, it may help to revise and edit a printed copy of your text – this can be particularly effective when trying to identify and resolve global problems in the text. When revising and editing, it is generally more efficient and effective to work systematically through the text. Flitting through the text, tweaking a sentence at the beginning, at the end and then in the middle, is, at best, a form of procrastination that leads to easier editing practices being completed while treatment of more serious issues is delayed or, even worse, never happens.

Feedback

An important aim of writing is for written words to communicate a particular message to the mind of the reader. After an appropriate amount of revision and editing, the best way of ensuring the achievement of this aim is to get someone to critically read your work. Feedback may identify where your writing style may need to be improved, whether some sections are difficult to understand, where contradictions occur or where the global structure might be improved. Don't take such criticism personally, although this is easier said than done; it may help your confidence to also ask about positive elements in your writing. It is important to ask your reader some questions that probe their understanding of the research content, just to check that their interpretation corresponds to the intended message. Try to receive criticisms in a spirit of gratitude: such feedback prevents a wider audience from detecting shortcomings in your writing.

More than likely, your supervisor will be a major source of feedback on your written work. You should both discuss the importance of effective writing and agree on the type of feedback that you need to improve your writing, and consider when and what types of feedback may be appropriate to the different types of writing that you produce (see Exercise 5.1).

Exercise 5.1

This exercise helps you to consider your expectations and needs from feedback on your work (writing, progress, research quality).

1   Before you submit written work to your supervisor:

   (a) Do you forewarn your supervisor that you will be submitting work?
   (b) Do you indicate the (approximate) amount of work to be submitted?

(c) Do you indicate by when you would like to have feedback provided?

2 When you submit written work to your supervisor, do you indicate what kind of feedback you are looking for?

(a) Do you indicate whether the feedback is required urgently or not?

(b) Are you specifically looking for comment on the research content only?

(c) Are you specifically looking for feedback on the quality of your writing?

(d) What balance do you expect between feedback on spelling and grammar, and feedback on the structure, logic and argument of your research?

(e) Which of the various editing practices (research content, global structure, layout and presentation, clarity of meaning, and so on) would you like your supervisor to focus on?

(f) Do you communicate these expectations to your supervisor?

3 On receipt of feedback, what do you do?

(a) Do you understand the feedback (written or oral) that your supervisor provides?

(b) When your supervisor provides feedback, are you clear about the criteria that they use to evaluate your work? List the criteria that you think they should use.

Ensure that your supervisor has ample time to read the thesis; otherwise, you will miss out on one of your single best sources of feedback. Do not put yourself, your supervisor or your thesis in a situation where the supervisor receives (without warning) the thesis content for the first time about ten days before the submission deadline (amazingly, there are instances when this occurs).

It may also be very rewarding to discuss the writing process with other research students: How do they recognise good writing? How do they attempt to improve their writing? What writing strategies work best for them? What feedback has helped their writing? How do they structure their thoughts as part of the writing process? What difficulties do they encounter when writing? What strategies do they use to overcome their difficulties?

Of course, your supervisor is not the only source of feedback available to you. Experienced writers tend to identify a 'critical friend' who is willing to read successive drafts of their work and provide constructive criticism and feedback (Hartley and Branthwaite 1989). If possible, identify a fellow research student who is willing to be a 'critical friend', and for whom you can return the favour. Indeed, once you get over any personal inhibitions about providing face-to-face feedback, the critical reading of other's work is a very powerful technique for learning to improve your own skills of editing and critical evaluation (Caffarella and Barnett 2000), as well as engaging in academic discourse (which contributes to preparation for an oral examination). An added advantage is that fellow students acting as a 'critical friend' will tend to return your work and provide feedback more promptly than your supervisor. They may also bring your writing up to a higher standard before submitting it to your supervisor, thereby allowing your supervisor to focus on more substantive issues of research content and global structure instead of editorial or formatting issues.

Completion of the thesis

The PhD programme is for a finite period, as is your funding. Therefore, there will come a point when you have to finish. For some this may be relatively easy, as experiments and surveys have been successfully completed. For many others, there may always be more research to be done – more literature to read and another experiment or survey that could clarify an issue. For others with an inclination to perfectionism, there may always be more improvements to be made when writing the thesis (see 'Thesis-writing for perfectionists' at www.services.unimelb.edu.au/llsu/pdf/otherpdfs/other009.pdf). As pointed out in Chapter 3, you need to plan the completion of your thesis as carefully as you did the design and execution of the research. As previously stated, to use a travel analogy, it can sometimes appear as if the destination of a PhD programme is the place where you are when you run out of fuel! It is difficult to provide general advice, but your supervisor will be an important source of guidance about whether you have conducted enough research and whether your thesis is of an acceptable standard for submission.

Murray (2002: Chapter 9) provides some further discussion on judging when you have done enough. She stresses that the thesis does not have to be perfect or brilliant but simply has to be 'good enough' for submission:

> Your work is good enough when:
> - your argument and conclusions are plausible, even if you are not completely happy with them;
> - your argument is convincing and coherent;
> - you have made a recognisable contribution to knowledge, even though you feel it is not earth-shattering;
> - you have made this visible in your introduction, conclusions and abstract, using the word 'contribution' or something very like it;
> - you have achieved some or all of the aims that you set out to achieve in your research and have reported this in your thesis;
> - feedback from your supervisor indicates that your work is adequate;
> - you have had publications – or even one – drawn from your research/thesis.
>
> (Murray 2002: 237)

The above points focus on the quality of the thesis, which is the overriding concern (see Chapter 7). Some students worry whether their thesis is long enough; however, any reader will prefer a thesis that does not have long, vague passages of text. Consider also the following (rather extreme!) example of the prominence of quality over quantity in the PhD thesis:

> Einstein completed his thesis at the end of April 1905, but he did not formally submit it to the University of Zurich until 20 July. The 21-page paper was soon accepted, although according to Einstein himself he was initially told that the thesis was too short; he added one sentence before resubmitting it, when it was promptly accepted.
>
> (White and Gribbin 1994: 80)

The written thesis is the prime focus of assessment

For examiners reading the PhD thesis and writing their examiner's report, first impressions count. From the moment the PhD examiner opens the envelope containing your thesis, they are consciously and unconsciously judging and assessing your thesis. Their first viewing of the thesis will be the title on the front cover, and their initial inspection of the thesis will take in the title page, the table of contents, the line spacing, font size, paragraph lengths, number of figures and tables, referencing style and, of course, the length of the thesis. Therefore – and this is a crucial point – it is your responsibility to write, structure and present the written thesis in a way that convincingly demonstrates research at doctoral level.

First impressions last

The reading of the thesis primarily determines the decision-making of the PhD examination. While this statement obviously applies in universities where a *viva* is not normally conducted, it also applies where a *viva* is usually conducted. A survey of UK universities found that examiners in the non-sciences (arts/humanities/social sciences) typically do not change their opinion of the thesis that is formed before the *viva*:

> Forty per cent of examiners . . . said that the decision about the thesis was made before the viva. In 74% of cases the viva served merely to confirm the examiners' opinions of the candidate . . . Where the viva did influence the examiners, this did not necessarily influence the examiners' decision.
>
> (Jackson and Tinkler 2001: 361)

Of course, the examiner's opinion of the thesis includes the content and quality of the research (discussed further in Chapters 1, 6 and 7). But issues associated with structure and presentation also significantly affect the examiner's overall opinion of the thesis, not least because such issues can profoundly improve the communication and comprehension of your doctoral research. Therefore, the examiner's first impression of the thesis is not simply achieved by the provision of a superficial 'polish': a positive first impression is achieved when the examiner detects the more substantial structural and presentational cues that will aid their reading and understanding of your doctoral research findings. For example:

> Never underestimate the importance of the presentation. No thesis with inadequate content will be accepted; but many theses, where the content is adequate, are dragged down into the borderline category by poor presentation.
>
> (Pratt 1984: 1114)

[T]he impression which examiners reach about the merit of a doctoral thesis is initially gained from the textual content and the presentation of the thesis.

(Trafford and Leshem 2002: 39)

Not surprisingly, examiners are negatively influenced when a thesis is not presented to a high standard:

Examiners quickly become annoyed and distracted by spelling, typographical, grammatical and referencing errors . . . One of the problems with work that is poorly presented is that the examiner tends to lose confidence in the candidate and can become suspicious that there are deeper problems of inadequate and rushed conceptualisation.

(Johnston 1997: 344, 345)

I give my students strong advice on how not to flip an examiner from being reasonable to unreasonable by having irritating things in the thesis such as typos and other careless textual mistakes that indicate lack of attention to detail. Once flipped (and I am aware of this happening), I am irritated and I have to work very hard at overcoming this irritation and not letting it influence my view of the thesis, although this is not easy.

(PhD examiner, quoted in Mullins and Kiley 2002: 378)

Examiners will base their assessment mostly on the research content of the thesis, but they need the research findings to be communicated adequately. Although a poorly presented thesis (that includes research of doctoral standard) is unlikely to result in a fail, it is certainly not in your interest (especially in borderline cases) to have presentational mistakes that 'flip' an examiner or lead them to suspect 'that there are deeper problems of inadequate and rushed conceptualisation' (Johnston 1997: 345).

Expectations of the examiners as readers

Thinking about the audience for your thesis highlights the role of the examiners as readers of the thesis; this challenges you to both consider and satisfy the needs and expectations of the examiners as readers. Statements in the previous section make it clear that examiners can be negatively affected by the presentation of the thesis: their expectations were not fulfilled. That the PhD examiner (or any other reader) has needs and expectations as a reader may not be immediately obvious:

> [T]he examiner approaches the reading of a thesis just like a reader of any new piece of writing. Examiners require all of the normal forms of assistance which should be provided to any reader. They appreciate work which is logically presented, focused, succinct, summarised and in which signposts are used to help readers to understand the path they are taking through the work.
>
> (Johnston 1997: 345)

> Seeing the examiner as a 'reader' is an important reminder. While examiners clearly bring the highest standards to their reading of the thesis, we cannot let this somehow release us from the responsibility of making our writing make sense to them . . . [T]hesis writers should see themselves as 'assisting' readers, not just persuading them, to see the value of their work.
>
> (Murray 2002: 54, 55)

Both these passages draw attention to the thesis writer's responsibility to 'signpost' and 'assist' the readers. Such 'signposting' and assistance will make your text more reader-friendly, and relevant techniques are discussed in a later section of this chapter.

Expectations of the examiners as examiners

Examiners will expect a variety of criteria to be satisfied in their reading of the thesis. A more detailed discussion of examiners' assessment criteria and practices is provided in Chapter 7, and should be read in conjunction with this section. In particular, you may find it useful to read the Institute of Education's criteria for examining a PhD thesis (see Box 7.1). It is important that your thesis is structured and presented to satisfy the examiners' expectations; in short, this means that the thesis must be written to display the characteristics and standards associated with a doctoral thesis (Chapters 1 and 7).

As you write your thesis, consider how its content addresses the standards and criteria that relate to doctoral research:

- Have you addressed all such issues (of relevance) in your thesis?
- Where exactly are these issues addressed in your thesis?
- Where does your thesis demonstrate that your research is of doctoral standard?

- Is it clear to the examiner that you are directly addressing these issues, or must the examiner infer and guess your intentions? (This is where forecasting and signposting may help.)

Some excellent examples of how PhD theses demonstrate the expected doctoral standards are provided by the University of Wollongong, Australia, in their website 'Thesis Writing Resources' (available at: http://www.uow.edu.au/research/current/thesiswriting.html). Advice is provided on the expected content from different sections of the thesis (e.g. abstract, literature review, results, discussion, conclusions) and an overview of the different types of thesis structure. Examples are included from all sections of the typical PhD thesis and across a range of disciplines. Each example is annotated to point out how the thesis meets the expected structure; issues of style are also discussed.

A fundamental aim of the PhD project is to provide a *research training* process that provides the research student with the skills to conduct research without supervision. Thus, the thesis should provide the examiners with insight into how you have learned to implement such skills to produce a project of doctoral standard. In practice, for example, this may mean that your written thesis should explain and justify the research approaches and methodology to a level of detail that exceeds that appropriate to a journal article. This expectation may not be so obvious. Doctoral students are under increasing pressure to publish their research, and their role models in a research discipline tend to be leading researchers who report their findings in journals in a very succinct and concise style. Writing a thesis, however, is not the same as writing for publication, and examiners (and other readers) expect a thesis to provide more information than would normally be presented in a journal publication (but this is not a licence to provide superfluous information). Even at universities where the publication of several papers is encouraged or required, it is generally not acceptable for the PhD thesis to consist of a selection of bound papers (published or unpublished). The bound papers must be accompanied by, for example, a general introduction and general discussion that seeks to integrate and synthesise the work so that it forms a coherent whole.

The structure and presentation of the thesis

A previous section mentioned the importance of 'issues of structure and presentation'. This section describes these issues in more detail, and their importance in achieving the expected standard of presentation. In this context, I discuss how university regulations impinge on the presentation of thesis, and highlight the use of typography as an aid to reading the thesis. I outline some common techniques that can assist readers, and briefly discuss and provide references for further reading for grammar, syntax and other conventions of academic writing.

Institutional requirements of theses

PhD examiners also inspect compliance with the university's formatting requirements for the thesis, and it should be a foregone conclusion that the required formatting has been correctly applied prior to submission. Your supervisor is responsible for ensuring that you are provided with the relevant information on the format of your thesis and submission deadlines. The details of these formatting requirements vary from university to university, but may also vary with time within a university; therefore, while it should be useful to inspect a recently submitted thesis from your university department, ensure that it is up to date. Typically, universities indicate requirements for the following:

- The title page. This is important. Most university departments have strict requirements for the format of the title page, which may include a sentence such as: 'Thesis submitted to the University of XYZ in candidature for the degree of Doctor of Philosophy.'
- Word limit for the Title
- Word limit for the Abstract
- Word or page limits for the thesis
- Paper size (typically A4), weight and colour
- Location of page numbers
- Table of contents
- Margin widths
- Font type and sizes (Times New Roman, 12 point is commonly used)
- Line-spacing of text
- Referencing style within the text and in the Bibliography
- Numbered headings
- Provision of raw data in the Appendices
- The provision of an electronic disk with raw data
- The type of binding that is required at submission (unbound, soft binding or hard binding)
- The number of thesis copies that must be submitted and to whom (may be a central university office rather than a departmental office).

Typographic layout

The layout of text (typography) can significantly affect people's ability to read and comprehend it (e.g. Hartley 1994a). For example, increased clarity and comprehension are associated with larger font size, the use of paragraphs, and some rewriting for clarification (see Hartley 1994b for further details).

A comparison of the two examples in Box 5.2 illustrates how a change in the layout of text and the use of some simple subheadings, font styles, line spacing and bullet points can improve the structure, presentation and clarity of a piece of writing. Example 2 in Box 5.2 is selected to illustrate the use of typography, but the majority of your thesis will not employ this number of typographical elements in such a short length of text; to do so would be very distracting for a reader. This example demonstrates the potential use of typography in some situations; however, the most common typographical issue in PhD theses is probably the division of long tracts of text into paragraphs with explanatory sub-headings.

Box 5.2 Typographical improvements to writing

Example 1

Identification of indicators for use in monitoring and evaluation of educational policies.

The objective of the study is to identify and select quantitative indicators for a monitoring programme that may be integrated into an evaluation of the effectiveness of educational policies. Overall, the work programme will: review the literature for information on current best practice in monitoring the impacts of educational policies; appoint a Steering Group that will advise on the ongoing development of the project, and conduct a consultation process with national experts, and with a number of stakeholder organisations with an interest in the monitoring of the impact and effectiveness of educational policies. The study will result in a report that will identify relevant and measurable environmental attributes, and significantly advance the ability to implement a monitoring programme. The study will not be directly addressing the design and implementation of a monitoring programme, which would require a detailed consideration of the sampling protocols, the experimental design of a sampling programme, and the data management and statistical treatment of the collected data.

Example 2

Identification of indicators for use in monitoring and evaluation of educational policies.

Objectives of the study

The objective of the study is to identify and select quantitative indicators for a monitoring programme that may be integrated into an evaluation of the effectiveness of educational policies.

Approach to the study

Overall, the work programme will:

- Review the literature for information on current best practice in monitoring the impacts of educational policies.
- Appoint a Steering Group that will advise on the ongoing development of the project.
- Conduct a consultation process with national experts, and with a number of stakeholder organisations with an interest in the monitoring of the impact and effectiveness of educational policies.

Scope of the study

The study *will* result in a report that will identify relevant and measurable indicators, and significantly advance the ability to implement a monitoring programme.

The study will *not* be directly addressing the design and implementation of a monitoring programme, which would require a detailed consideration of the sampling protocols, the experimental design of a sampling programme, and the data management and statistical treatment of the collected data.

As another example, a comparison of two abstracts that differ in their typographical layout is provided in Figure 1 of Hartley (2000) (which can be viewed online at http://www.pubmedcentral.nih.gov/article render.fcgi?artid=35254).

Techniques to assist the reader

As mentioned earlier, you will need to consider some techniques that assist the reader, and plan to implement these techniques appropriately. Examples of such techniques include forecasting, summarising, signalling and signposting (Murray 2002: 194). Overall, these techniques help the reader (including your examiners) to comprehend the coherence and storyline of the thesis.

Forecasting

Forecasting involves letting readers know in advance what will (or will not) happen in the text. Forecasting provides the reader with cues to allow them to 'set the scene'. An example would be a summary of the contents of a chapter; an overview at the beginning of a chapter that indicates the main issues and findings, or an indication of the sequence of events that occurs in a chapter, and how they contribute to the research question. An example of the latter (from a journal article in the social sciences) is as follows:

> The article looks first at what quantifiable measures may and may not tell us about the nature of madness in eighteenth-century Scotland and about the relationships between pathologies and the 'normal' structures of society. It seeks to test a common assumption or assertion, made by prominent figures such as Elaine Showalter, that 'madness is a female malady because it is experienced by more women than men'. It questions whether those with mental problems were really just the victims of an oppressive (professional and male) form of discourse. The second half of the article explores certain qualitative aspects of how insanity was construed by the sane, in order to assess the extent of gendering in the day-to-day under-standing of mental problems.
>
> (Houston 2002: 309–10)

Summarising

A related technique to forecasting is *summarising*, where the main message can be repeated at the end of a section. This can be a useful aid to achieve emphasis, and to remind the reader of the main message of the current section before they proceed to a new topic or section. It can also allow the reader to evaluate whether the preceding text supported your concluding main message, a preference indicated by a PhD examiner: 'I would suggest that a summary paragraph at the end of each section would give the reader an additional sense of priorities and focus and give the reader a what-did-it-all-mean type of understanding' (Johnston 1997: 340).

Signalling

Signalling involves the selection of words to display the various logical links in the research plan and to direct the readers' interpretation of your writing: 'it is not enough to have constructed a fine logical plan for your writing; it must be revealed for the readers' (Murray 2002: 197).

The use of comment and connecting words is advocated by Barrass (2002: 75) to 'help readers follow your train of thought'. Such comment words include 'clearly', 'even', 'as expected', and 'unexpected' and connecting words include: 'for example', 'first', 'second', 'if', 'then', 'even', 'therefore', 'hence', 'however', 'on the contrary', 'moreover', 'meanwhile', 'whereas', 'as a result', 'nevertheless', 'similarly', 'so', 'thus', 'but', 'either', 'or', 'on the one hand', and 'on the other hand' (modified from Barrass, ibid.). These comment and connecting words are important devices with which to convey more fully the meaning and interaction of sequences of logic in your text. For example, a contrast between two sequences of text can be achieved by the words 'however', 'on the contrary', 'alternatively' and 'but'; emphasis or clarification can be achieved by 'then', 'therefore', 'hence', 'moreover', and 'as a result'. The following extracts provide a further example, with the connecting words emphasised in bold:

> **While** countries where women have better education and economic opportunities have lower fertility in general, the directions of causality are not clear. **Perhaps** cultures that are ready to invest in educating girls and women are also ready for fertility to fall. **In any event,** in cultures where women are expected to marry early, raise many children and have no independent lives outside of their homes,

improving the status of women through education and employment overthrows the traditional concept of the family.

(Cohen 1995: 70–1)

Signposting

Signposting is similar to signalling; however, while signalling is embedded in the text, signposting usually operates at a higher level. Thus, signposting may be achieved by the use of headings, and subheadings (see Box 5.2 'Typographical improvements to writing'). Additionally, the first few sentences of a major section could be used to remind the reader of how that section contributes to the wider argument.

Overall, these (and other similar) techniques are a means of providing your readers with a framework to help negotiate the logical structure and organisation of your work and thereby better understand your research. Importantly, PhD examiners (and other readers) also value the benefits that arise from these techniques.

Exercise 5.2

Analyse a chapter of your own thesis or someone else's for the presence of:

- forecasting
- summarising
- signalling
- signposting.

Referring to the thesis chapter that you chose for analysis, could it have benefited from more use of these techniques? Identify which techniques would have improved specific sections.

Grammar and writing conventions

Examiners' reports almost always refer to writing quality and the editorial standard of the thesis (Johnston 1997: 339); examiners appreciate a well-written thesis, and they are negatively affected by a thesis with grammatical and editorial errors:

For my part, I found it very distracting and time-consuming to be continually stopping over things which should have been picked up before submission.

Finally, proper proof reading is required. There are word omissions, and words apparently left over from editing. Take care with sentence structure and with clarity of argument. The standard of literary presentation in the dissertation should be that of the journal and conference papers presented in support. At the moment, it is not.

One has to keep in mind that there is often a relationship between the quality of presentation and quality of scientific results.

(three examiners' quotes in Johnston 1997: 339, 340)

Sloppiness in the text indicates sloppy research.

(Mullins and Kiley 2002: 383)

These comments illustrate how a poorly written thesis can irritate an examiner, and undermine an examiner's confidence in the quality of the research. The second quote indicates the expected standard of writing – 'that of the journal'. Thus, your thesis is expected to demonstrate excellence in writing, as well as excellence in research.

Here, I have focused on the writing of text, but the presentation of your thesis is also likely to require some more specialised conventions, such as the presentation of tables and figures (and their legends), equations, statistical results, etc. Further reading on these topics will be readily available in your university library.

Does your writing need to improve if you are to attain a standard of excellence? If so, how will you achieve this improvement in your writing? Unless you are most fortunate, you will need to study and learn about writing. Of course, this is yet another demand on your time. In addition, the attainment of high quality in your writing requires time for drafting and numerous revisions. Unfortunately, many students choose not to allow time needed for learning about writing to compete with time for conducting research. However, this suggests that they neither fully appreciate that a good researcher needs to be a good writer nor that it is the quality, rather than quantity, of research that is important.

A variety of resources (online and printed) are available to help improve your writing. Many should be available in your university library and your supervisor may be able to direct you to resources of particular relevance to your discipline. Some recommended references on grammar and style are provided in the 'Recommended reading' section at the end of this chapter.

Referencing

Inconsistent and improper citation of references is frequently identified by examiners as an indicator of the poor quality of a thesis (Winter *et al.* 2000; Mullins and Kiley 2002). Therefore, I introduce some of the main conventions and practices associated with referencing.

Two common methods of referencing are the British Standard and the Harvard System. The British Standard method numbers the references in the order in which they are presented in the text. The examples in this chapter focus on the Harvard System. For some further information, see the resources of the Communication Skills Unit at the Bolton Institute (http://www.bolton.ac.uk/learning/pubs/csu/index.htm), and of the University of Liverpool's Graduate School ('Thesis Writing' at http://www.liv.ac.uk/gradschool/prdpresources.htm).

Note that the following information provides guidance on common conventions when citing references. However, your university may have more specialised requirements that conflict with the general guidance provided here – be sure to determine the correct referencing style that is required for your thesis.

Citing references in the text

One of the conventions associated with academic referencing is that any list of references that are cited in the text should be listed in chronological order. Thus, the first of these two examples is not correct; the second is:

1. For further information on the use of references in academic writing, see the following references in 'Selected reading': Day (1998), Lindsay (1995), Malmfors, Garnsworthy and Grossman (2000), Rudestam and Newton (1992: Chapter 4); Parsons and Knight (1995: 130–132), Hart (1998), Barnard, Gilbert and McGregor (2001) and Swetnam (1997).

2. For further information on the use of references in academic writing, see the following references in 'Selected reading': Rudestam and Newton (1992: Chapter 4); Lindsay (1995), Parsons and Knight (1995: 130–132), Swetnam (1997), Day (1998), Hart (1998),

Malmfors, Garnsworthy and Grossman (2000) and Barnard, Gilbert and McGregor (2001).

For references by one or two authors, the surnames of the author(s) are provided. For references with three authors, the three are referred to in full on the first mention, e.g. 'Malmfors, Garnsworthy and Grossman (2000)'. Subsequent references appear as 'Malmfors *et al.* (2000)'. Note that '*et al.*' usually appears in italics (because it is a Latin phrase) and with a full stop (because it is an abbreviation for *et alia*).

For references with more than three authors, only the first author is mentioned at all times in the text, followed by '*et al.*', e.g. Murphy *et al.* (2000). However, all of the authors in a multi-author paper must be listed in the References section.

The 'References' section

There are strict conventions surrounding the listing of references. Be very clear on the expected format for your thesis (if there is one), and consult with the requirements of your university. It is very important that you are absolutely consistent in your presentation of references. The main conventions are:

1   Alphabetically rank the surnames of first authors.
2   For each author, present their publications in order of single-author publications, double-author publications, and all other multi-author publications.
3   For each author, present their single-author publications chrono-logically from earliest to most recent publications; then for each double-author publication, rank chronologically from earliest to most recent publications; all other papers with more than two authors are then presented chronologically from earliest to most recent publications.
4   More than one publication in the same year by the same author(s) can be denoted alphabetically e.g. 2001a, 2001b, 2001c, etc.

Thus:
Anders, C. (2000)
Anders, D. (1987)
Anders, D. (2001)
Anders, D. and Franks, J. (1987)

Anders, D., Fatyer, F. and Franks, J. (1986)
Doody, A. (2002)
Doody, A., Patterson, D. and Franks, J. (2001a)
Doody, A., Patterson, D. and Franks, J. (2001b)

Exercise 5.3

In what order should the following list of authors be correctly presented in the References section?

Baker, J. and Adams, S. (1998)
Frank, A. and McCann, M. (1980)
Frank, A. (1987)
Gavin, B. (2000)
Adams, D. (2001)
Baker, J. (1999)
Andrews, D. (2000)
Baker, J., Adams, S. and Barrett, T. (1997)
Frank, G. (1985)

See Appendix 2 for the corrected version.

In the list of references at the end of your chapter/thesis, there must be an entry to match each of the references mentioned in the text. To ensure this, an excellent practice is to print off a hard copy of the text and the list of references. As you locate and identify references in the text, place a tick beside the corresponding entry in the list of references. If there is not a corresponding entry, then write in the author name, year of publication and page number of your text where this reference appears. When you are finished, your list of references will indicate which references need to be included. Any references without a tick are not mentioned in the text. At this stage, it may be useful to quickly double-check by using the 'Find' function of your word processor to check that the author's name does not appear in the text (however, this will not pick up any incorrect spellings of the name in the text). Then the reference either needs to be cited in the text or deleted.

Your university may prescribe the exact format of the references in theses. Otherwise, adopt one of the common formats, and *be absolutely consistent in your application of this format.* As an example of the different formats that may be encountered, consider the three variations of the following (fictional) reference: each of these variations uses the referencing format from a current journal.

Doody, A., Patterson, D. and Franks, J. (2001). What is a literature review? Journal of Postgraduate Education. 34, 23–35.

Doody, A., Patterson, D. and Franks, J. 2001. What is a literature review? *Journal of Postgraduate Education.* **34**: 23–35.

Doody, A., Patterson, D., Franks, J. (2001) What is a literature review? J. Postgrad. Educ. 34: 23–35.

It is essential that you proofread your thesis before submitting it. Although you will have been frequently told to proofread your thesis, it is possible that you will have had little prior experience of proofreading. Exercise 5.4 includes a number of common problems that appear in the References section of theses. This is a very realistic example: before proofreading, it is almost certain that your thesis will contain these types of error. I suggest that you photocopy this exercise and use a pen to circle the errors. Then (and only then!), compare your identification of the errors with the corrected version in Appendix 2. This exercise indicates how attentive to detail you need to be.

Exercise 5.4

This exercise illustrates common referencing problems, and provides some experience of proofreading.

There are several mistakes in the cited papers in the 'References' section below. How many can you identify?

The following reference provides the expected referencing format:

Lee, M. and Street, B. 1998. Student writing in higher education: an academic literacies approach. *Studies in Higher Education* **23**: 157–172.

References

Brent, E.E., 1986. The computer-assisted literature review. *Computers & the Social Sciences* 2: 137–151

Dewhurst, D. G., Macleod, H.A and Norris, T.A.M. 2000. Indpendent student learning aided by computers: an acceptable alternative to lectures? *Computers and Education* **35**, 223–241

Eklundh, K.S. 1994. Linear and non-linear strategies in computer-based writing. *Computers and Composition* **11**: 203–216.

Heinich, R. Molenda, M., Russell, J.D. & Smaldino, S.E. 1996. *Instructional Media and Technologies for Learning*. Englewood Cliffs: Prentice-Hall.

Szabo, A and Hastings. N. (2000). Using IT in the undergraduate classroom: should we replace the blackboard with PowerPoint? *Compters and Education* **35**: 175 – 187.

Marshall, S, 2001. Reference management software: it's your choice. *Technical Cmputing*, **22**; 16.

McGowan, Cynthia and Sendall, Patricia. 1997. Using the World Wide Web to enhance writing assignments in introductory chemistry courses. *J. Chem. Educ.* **74**: 391–392.

Conclusion

Writing is an important tool for developing your understanding; you should therefore write regularly and throughout the full duration of your doctoral programme – not just during the final six months. Writing the thesis in a way that convincingly demonstrates research of doctoral standard is easier said than done. The final submission of the thesis is often an emotionally tense and physically tiring experience and there may be added pressure to submit before a deadline. In this situation, it may be easy to lose sight of the fact that the submitted thesis is the prime object of assessment. Be careful not to submit a thesis that is sub-standard simply because it is rushed. Although the content and quality of your research may be of doctoral standard, excessive haste to meet a deadline may be at the expense of the time that is required to structure, write, revise and edit the thesis to a doctoral standard. Plan sufficient time for these important writing activities – they always require much more time than expected (printers fail, software incompatibilities arise, and you learn how to implement the correct formats). With appropriate planning throughout your writing and at the end of your doctoral programme, you will maintain and improve not just the quality of your research – which would be completed at this stage – but the quality of its presentation.

Recommended reading

Your library will contain many books on academic writing, and your supervisor can recommend some that will be most appropriate to your discipline. For researchers who may be non-scientists, note that much of what is termed 'scientific writing' is more widely applicable and should be more properly called 'academic writing'.

Publications

Barass, R. (2002) *Scientists Must Write: A Guide to Better Writing for Scientists, Engineers and Students*, 2nd edn, London: Routledge.

Booth, V. (1993) *Communicating in Science: Writing a Scientific Paper and Speaking at Scientific Meetings*, 2nd edn, Cambridge: Cambridge University Press.
Highly recommended.

Chambers, E. and Northedge, A. (1997) *The Arts Good Study Guide*, Milton Keynes: Open University Press.

Day, R.A. (1995) *Scientific English: A Guide for Scientists and Other Professionals*, 2nd edn, Phoenix, AZ: Oryx Press.

Day, R.A. (1998) *How to Write and Publish a Scientific Paper*, 5th edn, Westport, CT: Oryx Press.

Fabb, N. and Durant, A. (1993) *How to Write Essays, Dissertations and Theses in Literary Studies*, London: Longman.

Murray, R. (2002) *How to Write a Thesis*, Maidenhead: Open University Press.

Peat, J., Elliot, E., Baur, L. and Keena, V. (2002) *Scientific Writing: Easy When You Know How*, London: BMJ Books.

Swetnam, D. (1997) *Writing your Dissertation: How to Plan, Prepare and Present Your Work Successfully*, Oxford: How to Books.

Rudestam, K.E. and Newton, R.R. (eds) (1992) *Surviving your Dissertation: A Comprehensive Guide to Content and Process*, London: Sage.
See Chapter 9, 'Writing' by Jody Veroff.

Truss, L. (2003) *Eats, Shoots & Leaves: The Zero Tolerance Approach to Punctuation*, London: Profile Books.
An engaging and enjoyable introduction to punctuation.

Online resources

Thesis Writing Resources (University of Wollongong).
http://www.uow.edu.au/research/current/thesiswriting.html
This excellent site provides an overview of the different types of thesis structure, and includes examples from thesis chapters across a range of disciplines. Some issues of style are also discussed.

Paradigm Online Writing Assistant (POWA) by Chuck Guilford.
http://www.powa.org/
This is an interactive, menu-driven, online writer's guide and handbook.

'PhD: first thoughts to finished writing' by Katherine Samuelowicz, Lesley Chase and Mandy Symons, Learning Assistance Unit, University of Queensland, Australia.
http://www.tedi.uq.edu.au/phdwriting/

'How to write a PhD thesis' by Joe Wolfe, University of New South Wales.
http://www.phys.unsw.edu.au/~jw/thesis.html

A variety of excellent writing resources are provided by the Communication Skills Unit, The Bolton Institute.
http://www.bolton.ac.uk/learning/pubs/csu/index.htm

'Careful scientific writing: a guide for the nitpicker, the novice, and the nervous' by E.R. Firestone and S.B. Hooker.
http://www.stc.org/confproceed/2001/PDFs/STC48-000133.PDF

The Elements of Style by William Strunk.
http://www.bartleby.com/141/index.html

'Internet resources for scientific writing' by Svetla Baykoucheva.
http://pubs.acs.org/subscribe/journals/ci/31/special/02sb_inet.html
This website provides an impressive listing of a variety of Internet facilities that relate to scientific writing.

'Word usage in scientific writing'.
http://www.ag.iastate.edu/aginfo/checklist.html
This listing includes some of the troublesome words, terms, and expressions most frequently found in journal papers and bulletin manuscripts.

Scientific Training by Assignment for Research Students (STARS) by John Finn and Anne Crook.
http://www.ucc.ie/research/stars/links.html
A number of links to websites on plagiarism are available under the section 'Scientific Writing'. The links include examples of plagiarism and explanatory notes.

'Lawyer as writer' by James R. Elkins.
http://www.wvu.edu/~lawfac/jelkins/writeshop/links.html
Contains a variety of links about writing; see especially 'The Writing Process' 'Revising Your Writing' and 'Freewriting'.

Language and Learning Skills Unit, University of Melbourne.
http://www.services.unimelb.edu.au/llsu/resources/pg_materials.html
Provides essential reading on originality and thesis-writing for perfectionists, as well as external links.

Grammar, Punctuation and Capitalization: A Handbook for Technical Writers and Editors by M.K. McCaskill.
http://stipo.larc.nasa.gov/sp7084/index.html

Chapter 6

Publishing your research

Introduction

For any research discipline to progress and develop, new contributions to knowledge must be disseminated to the research community. To this end, researchers publish their research in many different ways: as conference abstracts, newspaper articles, popular articles in science magazines and bulletins, book chapters, etc. In some disciplines, it is common for the PhD thesis to be modified for publication as a book; however, publication in a research journal is typically the most important and influential method, because journal articles are reviewed by researchers with relevant expertise (a form of quality control) and are distributed to a specialist audience of scholars. In such a way, research is both open to critical evaluation and made available to the academic community.

In addition to disseminating knowledge, publication in a peer-reviewed journal is also important for PhD students, for a number of reasons. First, for many PhD students, the publication of several research papers is a formal requirement for the award of PhD degree (e.g. some universities in the Netherlands). For other students, there is more of an expectation of research papers, rather than a formal requirement. Nevertheless, a PhD thesis is usually required to demonstrate research of sufficient quality that, if written in a suitable form, would be publishable. Therefore, publication in an international peer-reviewed journal is clear and tangible evidence that your research meets the doctoral requirement to be publishable. Second, the publication of your research ensures its communication to the research community, both now and in the future. Through publication of your research and findings, you are directly engaging with, and becoming part of, the community of research scholarship. Publishing one's work also provides the possibility of receiving constructive feedback from other academics (Shaw and Abouzeid 2002). Third, the publication of your work establishes your claim for any credit and priority associated with the generation of new research (which may be particularly relevant in highly competitive research areas). Fourth, the successful publication of your work is recognition of the quality of your work, which develops your confidence, self-esteem and experience as a researcher. Of course, the publication of your research is also evidence to potential employers of your high-level training and ability in research.

Throughout this chapter, I describe some of the challenges and procedures associated with the publication of research, in the hope that these will be more manageable when you encounter them. However, publishing your research is not just about overcoming difficulties and learning procedures; more fundamentally, most researchers consider the publication of research to be an intellectually stimulating and rewarding experience. There is tremendous satisfaction in seeing your research reported in a journal, and a sense of completion about the work that was undertaken (indeed, many researchers consider that their research is not completed until it is published). Even experienced researchers who have published many papers continue to feel great pride and satisfaction from the publication of their work.

In this chapter, attention is focused on the typical process that occurs when a manuscript is submitted for publication in a peer-reviewed journal. By indicating the main stages in the publication process, I aim to demystify the process and boost your confidence as you prepare and approach this important milestone of your research career.

Deciding to publish

Although there may be clear benefits to publishing your work (see above), the demands of preparing a manuscript for publication mean that you need to consider whether publication is in your best interest. Publication of research will be more of a priority for students who intend to pursue an academic career. Similarly, student researchers in a rapidly developing area may need to publish as soon as possible: a two- or three-year wait until the thesis is completed may be too long. In contrast, students who are doing a PhD for personal development or intellectual challenge may well prefer to prioritise the completion of their thesis, keeping in mind that: 'It takes valuable time to write a manuscript for publication. It might be that this time could be better spent on the research studies' (Shaw and Abouzeid 2002: 61).

Discuss the publication of your work with your supervisor, and be realistic about whether the considerable time demands of the publication process are balanced by the benefits.

Preparing to publish

Many research students find the publication process daunting. However, there are several sources of assistance. Discuss the publication process with your supervisor and with other PhD students and postdoctoral researchers who are publishing their research. The guidance and experience of others can give you an insight into some of the requirements and demands of writing journal articles.

It is very likely that not all of your doctoral research will be publishable. Although sound in design, analysis and presentation, some research may not be of sufficient general interest or novelty to warrant publication in a journal. From an early stage, achieve great clarity on the research questions that you want to address in your research manuscript, and do not include other research of marginal relevance: include only the relevant research that is required to address the stated objectives. Students who first write up their research as a thesis chapter are often taken aback at how much more precision and focus are required to convert the chapter into a journal manuscript and reformat it in the journal's style. Therefore, be prepared to make the hard decisions to edit (and omit less relevant sections from) a thesis chapter that is being prepared for submission to a journal; it will save time and effort to do this sooner rather than later.

When publishing work from their thesis, it is typical that the research student is the lead author; this will entail some additional responsibilities: drafting the first version of the manuscript; distributing the manuscript to other authors for feedback and revision; incorporating comments from other authors into the manuscript; distributing the final version to all authors before submission of the manuscript to the journal; and ensuring that all authors agree to submit to the journal. It is worth clarifying who is responsible for the different activities right at the start of manuscript preparation, as supervisors sometimes undertake some of these.

Choosing a journal

It is advisable to identify an appropriate journal before you prepare a manuscript and your supervisor will provide valuable guidance in this respect. Nevertheless, by the time you have completed your manuscript (or maybe before you start writing it), you will probably have a reasonably good idea of two or three appropriate journals. Read the editorial policy of each of these journals (usually available on the journal's website) to ensure that your manuscript matches the subject area and scope of the journal. Check the typical length and style of the papers, and sample the titles and abstracts of some of the papers. You should soon get a good impression of whether your manuscript corresponds to the requirements of the journal.

When selecting a journal, you will need to consider a number of factors such as the duration between submission and publication, the degree of specialisation of the journal, whether page charges are applied, the rejection rate, whether it has a national or international circulation and whether the intended audience is composed of academics and/or practitioners.

Many professional evaluations of research performance use the impact factor of a journal as a measure of the quality of research output. Therefore, the impact factor is often an influential factor in the selection of a journal. The impact factor of a journal is a measure of the average frequency of citation of that journal's papers in one year. However, you should remember that a direct comparison of impact factors across different research categories is misleading; one simply cannot compare the circulation volume of *Nature* (with an impact factor of about 30) or *Annual Review of Biochemistry* (about 36) with *Death Studies* (about 0.7) or *Journal of Applied Psychology* (about 2). A more useful exercise may be to inspect the ranking of the journals within the subject category that is relevant to you. Despite the value of the impact factor, you can check whether you are publishing in the high-ranking journals within your research category. However, as stated above, the impact factor or ranking of the journal is only one of several considerations when choosing a journal.

Publish or perish

The pressures of the so-called 'publish or perish' principle have led to a strategy of some scientists deliberately publishing their work as 'minimum publishable units', thereby maximising the number of publications from their work. However, the content that is sufficient to satisfy a minimum publishable unit is usually only appropriate to less prestigious journals; in comparison, more prestigious journals will require considerably more content. A publication record of fewer papers in more prestigious journals is widely considered a better testament to a researcher's ability to conduct research of a high quality: 'Contributions to a scientific field are not counted in terms of the number of papers. They are counted in terms of significant differences in how science is understood' (NAS 1995). This is an important consideration for research students at the beginning of their careers, and who will inevitably be applying for research positions.

Authorship

Most of the time, the question of authorship (whose names should appear on the manuscript) is relatively easy to decide, and it is typical that the student's name is first. The important point is that you need to discuss and agree the issue of authorship with your supervisors (and any other potential co-authors) well in advance of producing a manuscript. Unfortunately, deciding on authorship can sometimes be awkward and occasionally controversial; when this occurs, disputes about authorship can be extremely divisive. Unfortunately, these situations can be difficult to resolve, and are becoming more frequent as more collaborative projects produce multi-author papers, and as researchers' professional performance is increasingly judged on publication output.

Problems with interpreting and applying authorship criteria are common. In a questionnaire returned by 809 corresponding authors of biomedical journal articles, 19 per cent of articles had evidence of honorary authors (named authors who did not meet authorship criteria), 11 per cent had evidence of ghost authors (individuals not named as authors but who had contributed substantially to the work), and 2 per cent had evidence of both (Flanagin *et al.* 1998). Therefore, about one in four articles in their sample demonstrated misapplication of authorship criteria and inappropriate assignment of authorship, which is 'incompatible with the principles, duties, and ethical responsibilities involved in scientific publication' (ibid.).

So, what set of criteria should be used to determine entitlement to authorship? Unfortunately, there is no universally agreed definition of authorship and, frequently, the absence of a common understanding about the criteria for authorship is the root cause of disputes. Box 6.1 'Further guidelines on authorship of journal publications' provides a more detailed account of criteria that are adopted by biomedical journals, and indicates the issues that surround entitlement to authorship. Even when criteria for authorship are well established, there may be difficulty in deciding when an individual fully satisfies the criteria – and there always are marginal cases. As if there is not enough confusion, it seems there are few institutional mechanisms, protocols or conventions that provide detailed guidance on either allocating authorship or resolving disputes.

PhD students whose manuscript is at issue may find themselves in the difficult, if not intolerable, position of trying to mediate between senior researchers. The situation calls for a steady temperament and, if initial efforts do not resolve the situation, it is highly advisable to seek some form of arbitration by a senior figure, such as the person responsible for postgraduate students or the Head of Department.

When a dispute arises, journal editors do not normally get involved – disputes about authorship (or any other issue) need to be resolved before submitting a manuscript to a journal. However, issues may arise after submission, e.g. a student becomes aware that their supervisor has submitted a manuscript that is based on the student's work, but which does not include the student as an author. In such a (rare) case, you must inform the journal editor as soon as possible, as such issues can be more easily dealt with before publication. For a manuscript that has been accepted but not published, then it is most likely that it will not proceed to publication until the authors come to an agreement. If they cannot, one possibility is for each author to submit their case to the journal, and the journal editors could act as an impartial panel; however, this would be quite an exceptional occurrence. If the manuscript has already been published, a similar form of arbitration can be used. If the decision is to make changes to the authorship of a published paper, then a note would have to be published in the journal, pointing out the changes. The Institute for Scientific Information (ISI) would be notified and asked to correct their files, and changes would have to be made to the journal's website files.

Box 6.1 Further guidelines on authorship of journal publications

The 'Vancouver Protocol' establishes guidelines for the format of manuscripts submitted to a large collection of biomedical journals, and is set out in the fifth edition of the Uniform Requirements for Manuscripts Submitted to Biomedical Journals (http://www.icmje.org/). It covers a variety of issues that relate to style, format, ethical conduct, and responsible research practices. The 'Vancouver Protocol' provides the following minimum requirements for authorship:

> All persons designated as authors should qualify for authorship, and all those who qualify should be listed. Each author

should have participated sufficiently in the work to take public responsibility for appropriate portions of the content. One or more authors should take responsibility for the integrity of the work as a whole, from inception to published article. Authorship credit should be based only on:

1 substantial contributions to conception and design, or acquisition of data, or analysis and interpretation of data;
2 drafting the article or revising it critically for important intellectual content;
3 final approval of the version to be published.

Conditions 1, 2, and 3 must all be met. Acquisition of funding, the collection of data, or general supervision of the research group, by themselves, do not justify authorship.

Authors should provide a description of what each contributed, and editors should publish that information. All others who contributed to the work who are not authors should be named in the Acknowledgments, and what they did should be described.

Increasingly, authorship of multicenter trials is attributed to a group. All members of the group who are named as authors should fully meet the above criteria for authorship. Group members who do not meet these criteria should be listed, with their permission, in the Acknowledgments or in an appendix (see Acknowledgments).

The order of authorship on the byline should be a joint decision of the coauthors. Authors should be prepared to explain the order in which authors are listed.

In addition to a variety of recommended practices for research projects, the Danish Committee on Scientific Dishonesty provides detailed discussion on the Vancouver Protocol and other authorship issues in 'Guidelines for Good Scientific Practice (1998)', available at http://www.forsk.dk/eng/uvvu/publ/. A number of useful publications and resources are also available from the Committee on Publication Ethics at http://www.publicationethics.org.uk/.

Submitting the manuscript

Having identified a journal, your manuscript needs to conform to the 'Instructions for Authors' that are typically available on the inside cover of the journal and on the journal's website. Make sure that you show the manuscript to each of the co-authors (if there are co-authors). You should expect significant feedback from your supervisors, not just on grammar, but also on the research issues, methodology, results and interpretation. After incorporating their comments, and when you think the manuscript is ready to send to the journal, it is a very good idea to put the manuscript away for a while, and then re-read and proofread it. You will inevitably find mistakes or wish to make improvements.

Do not blindly incorporate the feedback and comments of your supervisor and co-authors. The majority of their comments will be helpful, but if you are doubtful about any point that they have made, it is very important that this is discussed and a consensus is attained. By the time you begin to publish your research, you will have acquired significant expertise and should be more knowledgeable about the specific details of your research topic than your supervisor and co-authors; therefore, you should be ready to take responsibility for explaining, clarifying and resolving any differences in interpretation that arise. It is crucial that your manuscript is written and presented to the highest possible standard before it is submitted to the journal; specifically, do not look upon the journal refereeing system as a double-check on your work – poorly written manuscripts will be quickly rejected by busy referees and editors.

Having ensured that all authors have seen the final version of the manuscript and agree to submit it, the next step is to submit the required number of copies to the journal. When submitting a manuscript for publication, it is conventional to submit the text only as one single section. A separate page is next provided for all of the figure legends, followed by each of the figures on a separate page. Each table (with the appropriate legend above the table) is presented on a separate page. Make sure that you have printed a high quality copy of the text, figures and tables. It is usual to include a cover letter that simply provides the manuscript title and authors, and indicates that you will expect to hear from the journal editor in due course.

When deciding who is corresponding author, it is worth considering that the supervisor will usually be at the same address for a period of years, whereas research students may not. Note that the time between submission of the manuscript and seeing your paper in print can be considerable, and can vary from 6 months to 18 months. You will feel, deservedly, a huge sense of relief when you submit the manuscript. However, in most cases, there will still be plenty of work to be done in light of the referees' comments.

The publishing of journals is undergoing many changes to accommodate and benefit from electronic media. Some journals currently permit electronic submission of journals, a practice that is likely to become more widespread in future. Many journals now have an electronic tracking system that allows an author to track the progress of their manuscript from submission to refereeing to publication.

The peer-review process

Upon receipt of the manuscript, the journal will typically acknowledge receipt and provide you with a reference, which you should use in all correspondence. The journal editor next sends a copy of the manuscript to (typically) two referees a.k.a. reviewers. The referees are involved to ensure that your manuscript is suitable to the scope of the journal, contains research of an acceptable standard, and, if appropriate, to suggest improvements to the manuscript. The content and form of referees' reports vary across journals. Many journal report forms have criteria that are used to guide the evaluation. It is worth asking your supervisor about the conventions and criteria that may be associated with your research discipline. It is remarkable how similar the assessment criteria used by the journals of very different research disciplines may be; examples of common assessment criteria are provided in Box 6.2.

Box 6.2 Overview of prominent criteria used to assess journal manuscripts

Presentation

Does the title of the paper clearly reflect the contents?
Does the abstract represent the contents of the paper, and is it informative rather than merely indicative?
Is the text clear and well written?
Is the paper unnecessarily long?
Are all the tables and figures necessary, and are the legends sufficiently informative?

Do all the tables and figures present the data accurately and
  effectively?
Is the paper accessible to both specialists and non-specialists with
  an interest in the topic, or is it accessible to specialists only?

Content

Is the research put in the context of the research field as a whole?
Are the objectives/hypotheses clearly stated?
Are the ideas soundly developed and clearly presented?
Is the methodology clearly stated and appropriate to the objectives?
Is the statistical treatment adequate and are the data correctly
  interpreted?
Are the conclusions justified?
Is the paper sufficiently rigorous, accurate and correct?
Is conflicting evidence overlooked or ignored?
Are key references included and are the references up to date?

Importance

Is the research of major significance on an important or highly
  novel topic?
Is the research of broad significance with some novel aspects?
Is the research useful but lacking in originality: sound but routine?
Is the research of limited significance?
Is the research outside the scope of the journal?

Overall assessment

Overall assessment: excellent/good/weak?
Are the interpretations and conclusions sound and justified by the
  evidence/data?
Is this a new and original contribution?
Does it give sufficient attention to the literature?

Recommendation

Accept without revision.
Accept with minor editorial changes.

Accept with revision, but not requiring reconsideration by the referees.

Review again after major revision.

Reject in present form but encourage submission of new manuscript.

Reject without prospect of resubmission.

Is there any reason for rapid publication?

The provision of a written evaluation from the referees is an almost universal feature of the peer-review process. The content and tone of some referees' comments are legendary – unfortunately, this is because of the sometimes rude and personal nature of the comments (which a good journal editor should not tolerate), and other times dogmatic and blunt approach. However, the majority of referees are professional, helpful and well intentioned and, as a general rule, you should expect them to be tough but fair. It is almost inevitable that the referees will provide some criticism, albeit in a constructive manner. Ultimately, their comments will improve the quality of your publication. For example, comments may point out instances of poor presentation, misrepresentation of other research findings, problems with references, a request for clarification of certain points (most often in the Objectives, Materials and Methods or Discussion), or a request for less relevant text to be deleted (see Box 6.4). Most of these issues can be dealt with as minor revision. However, referees may request major revisions as a condition of publication, e.g. they may insist upon a different analysis of data (with the consequent effects on the Results and Discussion and Conclusion of the manuscript), redrawing of graphs and tables, restructuring of the manuscript, or a substantial reduction in length.

Of course, referees may also recommend that the manuscript is not suitable for publication; however, there may be a number of reasons for this. For example, the manuscript may be of a perfectly acceptable standard, but not appropriate to the scope of the journal that you sent it to. As another example, the manuscript is rejected, but may be recommended for resubmission after major revision. Alternatively, the manuscript is rejected because the research or its reporting is not of an acceptable standard. For research students submitting their work for publication, it can be a disheartening or even devastating experience to have their work rejected. Although rejection is not easy to take, don't worry; you are in good company. Virtually all researchers have had manuscripts rejected, and a study of successful ecologists found that almost one quarter of their published papers were rejected at least once: 'However, manuscript rejection is not indicative of scientific inadequacy ... The moral seems to be that if at first you don't succeed, try try again' (Cassey and Blackburn 2003: 376).

In an analysis of 142 reviews of 58 manuscripts received by an educational journal, the following broad categories of referees' criticisms were identified, in order of frequency of occurrence:

- lack of methodological transparency, adequacy or rationale;
- unjustified claims;
- shortcomings in format;
- theoretical shortcomings;
- data analysis problems;
- inadequacies in literature reviews;
- insufficient clarity of focus;
- conceptual confusion;
- parochial blinkers (manuscripts needed to make the local nature of their research, or their terminology, more meaningful for a wider audience);
- does not add to the international research literature;
- failure to link findings to the research literature;
- lack of critical reflection on implicit assumptions;
- victory claims (overly optimistic or totally positive reporting that needed to acknowledge the complexity and diversity in the data).

(Alton-Lee 1998: 888–90)

Given the confidential and personal nature of the peer-review process, it is not surprising that research students rarely see referees' reports on others' work (but see Cambridge 1994). Here, I provide a complete referee's report following the submission of a manuscript to an educational journal. The manuscript described the educational aims of a website that was designed to assist the development of students' research skills. For reasons that will become obvious, the manuscript was eventually published elsewhere (Finn and Crook 2003, http://bio.ltsn.ac.uk/journal/vol2/index.htm) and it may be useful to view it in order to fully appreciate the comments.

Box 6.3 Example of a referee's report

The following is an extract from a report (by the editor, in this case) on a manuscript submitted to an educational journal in the UK.

May I first thank you very much for your paper. How we deal with helping students to prepare for any piece of research, whether at UG, PG or PhD level is a fascinating topic, and the points that you raise are food for thought. I have looked at the website, and it is good to see that you have put such material online for learners. There are some very good exercises, and some useful reading about the matter. Putting online what should (but perhaps is not always!) be done by us, as lecturers, prior to the students starting their final year project is good practice indeed . . .

. . . But, back to the paper more generally. It appears to me that this is a description of how you put online the material that, in most disciplines I guess, is provided by way of seminars, handouts and the like. And, in various ways, and with varying degrees of success (whatever success means) our learners somehow get their final year project done. In its current format, this paper is in essence a report on what you did to make available, via the web, the material/exercises that form part of a normal module/course. As yet, it is not quite a description of a piece of research and, for a more 'traditional' journal such as ours, papers normally describe a piece of research.

. . . That said, there is a paper waiting to emerge here! It is just that you have submitted it too early! At the moment it is a description of (very good) practice. In order to turn it into something more 'research-y', you need to address the very issue that you raise in the last paragraph, that is, to provide *evidence* that such a system is an effective learning aid. For this, you need to *measure* it in some way. So, it would be great to monitor the use of your online material, and to compare performance (but not just of marks; that would be too narrow a view of 'success') of learners who have used the system against the performance of those who did not (students from previous years). Or, perhaps, look at what kind(s) of students use such a system. As an example, do more males than females use it, and in what way(s)? Do older/younger students access/use it more? Does background influence its use? What exercises did students use more than others? One hypothesis (of many) could thus be something along the lines of 'would the performance of students' x, y and z skills be improved by their use of such a system?' (And in what way?) Evidence could be gathered from monitoring use of the system itself, from students, and from supervisors, of course. The literature review would thus need to be much more focused on what we know/do not know about such skills, rather than, at present, making the argument for Computer Aided Learning (CAL). The argument for CAL has already been made (it is widely used); we now need to scope down and say how, precisely, it helps/does not. I would also suggest that you omit the science/non-science education bit; this takes you off track (and is another paper entirely).

I am therefore very sorry to say that, given that the research is not yet done, your paper cannot be considered for possible publication in the Journal. That said, I would be very interested to look at any study you do at a later date. Given the sheer volume of articles submitted to the Journal for consideration, we are now having to reject more than three-quarters of these. Many would regard this as an accolade for the Journal in that it shows that we are able to select very high quality material, but I know that this also has a human cost.

I trust that this will not deter you from writing further articles and submitting them to the journal in the future. Once again, may I thank you for your article.

Exercise 6.1

1   Why was the manuscript discussed in Box 6.3 rejected?
2   Were there obvious reasons for the rejection?
3   How would you describe the tone of this report?

The above example is particularly polite, and there is a considerable level of constructive and helpful criticism. Not all referees are so polite in their reports; however, the provision of constructive criticism is not unusual, even for a rejected manuscript. Of course, not all referees will take (or have) the time for this level of feedback, but the chances of getting such useful feedback are reduced if the submitted manuscript is poorly prepared and of low quality.

The following extracts are from five different reports that I have either written as a referee or received; I provide them to give some other examples of the deciding factors behind the assessment of these manuscripts, and a wider sample of the tone of reports. Although these extracts are from assessments of ecological research, many of the core criticisms are generic in their applicability (see Alton-Lee 1998).

Box 6.4 Selected extracts from several referees' reports

Example 1

No hypotheses are presented, which hinders an evaluation of the research. In general, I am not at all convinced by the chain of inference in the discussion. The conclusions rest on a reasonably small data set in one location, and are quite speculative. At the very least, a much more cautious tone should be present. The title is not appropriate and should be far more modest. Overall, this is a very descriptive piece of research that will only be of interest to a specialist audience. As such, and with some improvements, the manuscript is more suited to another journal. Nevertheless, I hope that the authors may benefit from the following comments: . . .

Example 2

Overall, I consider that this paper makes a positive contribution to this research topic, and improves understanding of the processes and associated methodology. Given the potentially contentious nature of this research, I would strongly suggest that some extra information is provided that anticipates potential doubts/criticisms. For example, in Section 2.2, please provide assurance that the animals had not received any parasiticide treatment in previous 6 months/12 months (or whatever period is appropriate). In the same section, provide some form of assurance that the three separate paddocks received consistent management prior to and during the experiments (or some other appropriate statement), e.g.

---

that feeding regimes, grass composition and soils, etc. were 'substantially equivalent' across the three paddocks. This would help overcome suspicion that differences amongst the three paddocks were responsible for the treatment differences.

Example 3

I find this paper to be a premature reporting of results that require more detailed data to support the conclusions. It seems that a major motivation for this paper centres about whether the food source is a 'rare' or 'common' resource. Unfortunately, there are no data presented with which to evaluate the rarity or otherwise of the food resource. I am somewhat sceptical of the generality of the results that are presented, given the single sampling occasion, and the renowned heterogeneity in such data sets.

Specific comments:

- The Introduction needs to explain more clearly what is the hypothesis under investigation, and why the investigation is of importance.
- Some indication of the approximate size of the different resource types should be provided.
- In some parts, the English needs improving.
- Table 1: the reader should, *at least*, be able to determine the sample size of each category that was sampled.
- Table 2: round off values to nearest integer ('percentage' incorrectly spelled in legend).

Example 4

This manuscript addresses an important topic. As I have worked on the question myself, I can confirm that the one question always to surface after a talk is to what extent these ecological processes are likely to reflect the influence of competition. This manuscript will keep me from shrugging my shoulders. The authors make an excellent job in summarising available knowledge: I find their text timely, concise and suitably critical. Nevertheless, I have a few queries, which I have listed in perceived order of importance . . .

Example 5

The study contains a large amount of data that should be of considerable interest to a specialist group. Indeed, following some revision, I consider that the paper is better suited for publication in another journal . . . There should be clearly stated hypotheses in the Introduction, not just aims. The Results (and some of the Discussion) section is detail-laden and presented in a largely undigested form, and needs to be condensed for publication. There are parts that have a very selective presentation of the results and statistics, e.g. focusing on the significant differences only. . . . The aims of some of the statistical analyses need to be stated more explicitly. . . . The Figure and Table legends should be more explanatory.

The journal editor will forward the referees' comments to the corresponding author. The editor will inform you whether the manuscript is accepted with no, minor or major revision, or may politely decline to accept the manuscript. At this point, you may feel elated, devastated or, more usually, somewhere in-between.

If you are unhappy with the response, don't do anything rash! Read the referees' comments thoroughly, put them aside for a day or two and read them again. If both referees make the same points, then you will have to address these points fully, and most points that referees make will be valid and useful in improving the quality of your manuscript. When the referees disagree in their recommendations, the editor may either make a decision or send the manuscript to another referee. However, it is reasonably common that a referee may misinterpret a point, and consequently may make what you consider to be an inappropriate request or suggestion. In such cases, you are entitled to (politely!) point this out to the editor, and you should indicate where you have modified the text to avoid a repeat of such a misunderstanding. Don't respond to the editor without all co-authors having agreed on the content of the reply to the editor, and having agreed to all changes to the original manuscript.

See Bem (1995, available at http://comp9.psych.cornell.edu/dbem/psych_bull.html) for further discussion and some examples of the right and wrong way to respond to referees' comments (see also Box 6.5). A reproduction of the correspondence between an author, two referees and the editor of the *Journal of Teaching Writing* provides further examples of academic discourse that occurs among these different groups as part of the publication of a manuscript (Cambridge 1994).

Box 6.5 Responses to referee's comments

The following extract from Bem (1995) gives an example of two very different responses to a referee's comments:

Wrong approach: 'Reviewer A is obviously Melanie Grimes, who has never liked me or my work. If she really thinks that behaviorist principles solve all the problems of obsessive-compulsive disorders, then let her write her own review. Mine is about the cognitive processes involved.'

Right approach: 'As the critical remarks by Reviewer A indicate, this is a contentious area, with different theorists staking out strong positions. Apparently I did not make it clear that my review was intended only to cover the cognitive processes involved in obsessive-compulsive disorders and not to engage the debate between cognitive and behavioral approaches. To clarify this, I have now included the word "cognitive" in both the title and abstract, taken note of the debate in my introduction, and stated explicitly that the review will not undertake a comparative review of the two approaches. I hope this is satisfactory.'

Publication

Having made the necessary revisions and assuming that the resubmitted manuscript has been accepted for publication, the manuscript goes to the publishers. Some time after submission, 'galley proofs' of the journal article will be posted or emailed to the corresponding author. Galley proofs are a draft version of how the article will appear in the journal. It is very important that you meticulously proofread the galley proofs – any mistakes that remain will appear in the printed version, for every reader to see. At this stage, you will have an opportunity to correct any minor typographical or grammatical errors that were in the final submission. However, you need to be vigilant for errors that may have been introduced during the typesetting process. These can be quite subtle, e.g. a comma is replaced by an apostrophe, a semi-colon disappears, notation in an equation may not be correct (potentially disastrous), references may not appear in the References section, or a letter may disappear from a word. Pay particular attention to tables, figures and their legends. To be fair, these mistakes are very rare; however, this makes them more difficult to detect. The editors and typesetters are far more likely to find your mistakes that were in the submitted manuscript.

After the corresponding author receives the galley proofs, a quick response is usually required, e.g. publishers request that you return the proofs and any corrections within 2–4 days. The article is now 'in press'.

After returning the galley proofs and any necessary corrections, the article will appear in the journal soon after (from weeks to months). A few weeks after publication, the corresponding author will receive a number of offprints (copies of the article) from the journal, as indicated in their 'Instructions to Authors'. Some journals provide a limited number (e.g. 25–50) of offprints for free, whereas others will require payment. Other researchers with an interest in your work are likely to request offprints from the corresponding author. You should provide all of the co-authors with some offprints, and it is courteous to send a copy to individuals who assisted with the work.

Conclusion

Remember that journals need a supply of manuscripts. If you can produce a manuscript that competently describes good quality research that falls within the scope of the journal, then you are quite likely to get your manuscript published. Note the 'If' in the preceding sentence. It is important that you can write and present data appropriately, are aware of what constitutes research 'quality' and select a suitable journal. It may be hard to believe if you are about to write your first paper, but by the time you publish your third or fourth paper you will be much more at ease with the protocols of publishing, and more focused on the research content of the manuscript – and enjoying the publication of your research.

Recommended reading

Publications

Berry, R. (1986) *How to Write a Research Paper*, Oxford: Pergamon.

Booth, V. (1993) *Communicating in Science: Writing a Scientific Paper and Speaking at Scientific Meetings*, 2nd edn, Cambridge: Cambridge University Press. Highly recommended, and applicable to most research disciplines.

Day, R.A. (1998) *How to Write and Publish a Scientific Paper*, 5th edn, Westport, CT: Oryx Press.

Online resources

'Writing articles for scientific journals: a basic guide' by J. W. Stirling. http://www.aims.org.au/journal/write.html

'How to write a scholarly research report', online journal article by Lawrence M. Rudner and William D. Schafer (1999) *Practical Assessment, Research & Evaluation*, 6: article 13. http://pareonline.net/getvn.asp?v=6&n=13

'Authorship ethics' by K.L. Syrett and L.M. Rudner (1996) *Practical Assessment, Research & Evaluation*, vol. 5, article 1. http://PAREonline.net/getvn.asp?v=5&n=1

'The ethics of authorship: does it take a village to write a paper?' by Glenn McGee. http://nextwave.sciencemag.org/cgi/content/full/2001/03/28/7

'How to handle authorship disputes: a guide for new researchers' by Tim Albert and Elizabeth Wager. http://www.publicationethics.org.uk/cope2003/pages2003/AdvicetoAuthors.pdf

Chapter 7

The PhD examination process

Introduction

In Chapter 1, the expected standard of the PhD degree was discussed. This chapter focuses on the actual examination practices and criteria that are used by examiners to judge whether the requirements for the award of a PhD have been satisfied. Your awareness of the practices of PhD examiners is important: as a candidate for the PhD examination, you need to know the criteria with which PhD examiners assess your doctoral research. Such knowledge will make you further aware of the standards that your research and thesis must attain.

In this chapter, I provide an overview of the different aims of the PhD examination and the examination process. I draw attention to the dominant role of the thesis in the PhD examination, even when an oral examination (*viva*) is held. I discuss the examination practices and criteria adopted by examiners as they assess both the thesis and the *viva*.

Aims of the PhD examination

Although the PhD examination provides a single result, the process can be comprised of two parts: (a) the examiners' reading of the thesis; and (b) the oral examination. Some universities do not normally conduct an oral examination; however, for the purposes of this chapter, I assume that an oral examination will be conducted.

Overall, the PhD examination is intended to do the following:

- ensure that the institutional requirements of the thesis are satisfied (for example, the correct format and presentation have been adopted);
- ensure that the work has been conducted by the candidate;

- ensure that the thesis demonstrates an original contribution to knowledge;
- ensure that the candidate has a thorough understanding of the concepts, theories, methodologies and applications (where appropriate) of their subject;
- ensure that the candidate is aware of how the thesis advances their subject;
- ensure either that the research is of sufficient quality to be potentially publishable, or, where publication is a requirement, ensure the research has been published;
- assess (grade) the candidate's thesis;
- provide discussion and feedback that may help improve the work for subsequent publication;
- acknowledge the candidate's entry to a community of scholarship (most relevant where a *viva* occurs).

The ultimate aim of the PhD examination is to judge whether the candidate is capable of independently conducting high quality research: 'Above all, examiners tend to want to be satisfied that the researcher has become an expert in the chosen field and has demonstrated competence to do the kind of research that s/he set out to do' (Lawton 1997: 17).

The examination process

One of the common features of the examination process is the appointment of an external examiner who usually plays a dominant role in the examination of the PhD. The external examiner is typically selected on the basis of criteria that relate to academic credentials, research experience, experience in examining and independence (Tinkler and Jackson 2000). As might be expected, there is considerable variation in the extent to which the selection criteria of the external examiner are stated in university regulations and interpreted by academics. Nevertheless, the intention of such regulations is: 'the fostering of impartiality, the preservation of common academic standards and the making and performance of community' (ibid.: 172). In addition to the external examiner, at least one internal examiner is usually appointed from your university department.

The following is a description (from an Australian study) of how examiners typically deal with a thesis that is sent to them:

[D]ifferent examiners approach the task differently, but most examiners begin by reading the abstract, introduction and conclusion to gauge the scope of the work, and by looking at the references to see what sources have been used and whether they need to follow up on any of them. They then read from cover to cover, taking detailed notes, and finally go back over the thesis to check on whether their questions have been answered or whether their criticisms are justified.

(Mullins and Kiley 2002: 376)

The important output from the examiners' reading of the thesis is a report on the thesis from each examiner. Each examiner also comments on the candidate's thesis under a number of categories. Although the categories will depend on the university's specific criteria, these typically include: the presentation of the thesis, originality, contribution to knowledge, evidence of critical thinking and evidence of publishable material. In addition, the examiner's report usually provides a provisional recommendation on the grade of the thesis. The examiners' reports are submitted (usually independently) to the appropriate university committee.

The *viva* takes place some time after the examiners' reports have been submitted. Following the *viva*, the examiners submit a joint report or, if they cannot agree, separate reports.

The details of the examination process display considerable variation across universities, and it is imperative that you know the process that operates in your university. Your supervisor will be an important source of guidance (see also Exercises 7.1, 7.2 and 7.3).

Exercise 7.1

This exercise aims to heighten your awareness of the submission and examination process for the thesis.

Discuss the examination process with your supervisor. The following questions may help guide the discussion:

1   Do I have a copy of the university documents that stipulate the regulations regarding the submission of theses and do I fully understand them?

2   Have I obtained a copy of any available guidance to PhD examiners or the template for the examiner's report form?
3   When are the deadlines for the submission of theses?
4   Where do I submit the thesis?
5   How many copies must be submitted?
6   What accompanying documentation will be required?
7   Is there an examination fee, and how much is it?

The thesis is the main focus of assessment

When discussing the examination of the PhD, many of your fellow students and other researchers may focus their discussions on the oral examination; this is not surprising as many students are understandably anxious about the *viva* (usually more because of a fear of the unknown rather than fear of failing). The oral examination is prominent in the minds of PhD candidates, because the face-to-face and immediate nature of the *viva* makes it a more intense emotional experience than the submission of the thesis.

However, a word of caution is in order. *The crucial examination of your PhD candidacy is that of the thesis, not the* viva. This point was raised in Chapter 5 in the context of the impact of structure and presentation of the thesis on an examiner. It is worth reiterating the research finding that most examiners do not change their opinion of the thesis that is formed before the *viva*:

> Forty per cent of examiners . . . said that the decision about the thesis was made before the *viva*. In 74% of cases the *viva* served merely to confirm the examiners' opinions of the candidate. . . . Where the *viva* did influence the examiners, this did not necessarily influence the examiners' decision.
>
> (Jackson and Tinkler 2001: 361)

Jackson and Tinkler's (2001) finding was based on the experience of examiners in the social sciences. However, I suggest that the examination process indicates that the importance of the thesis prevails across a variety of disciplines. A revealing insight is that *on the basis of the thesis alone*, examiners produce a report and make a recommendation on the outcome of the result. Therefore, regardless of the degree of importance attached to the *viva*, an examiner's reading of the thesis cannot fail to govern their approach to the *viva*. This conclusion is 'based upon logic rather than evidence' (Trafford and Leshem 2002: 40). For example, based on the thesis, the examiner will approach the oral examination with an impression that the candidate is a clear fail, a clear pass or a borderline case. It is probably in the latter case that the *viva* makes the greatest contribution to determining the awarded grade:

> The decision as to whether or not the thesis is up to the required standard is tentatively taken before the oral examination. However, a poor performance in the oral may lead the examiners to question their decision, while a good performance can boost an unfavourable one into a pass.
>
> (Cryer 2000: 239)

Therefore, while you must take the *viva* seriously and prepare adequately for it as an examination, it is more important that you first submit your written thesis with a clear understanding that it is the thesis that will dominate the assessment of your doctoral research.

What are the examination criteria?

The judgement of the PhD examiner will always remain an important element of the examination process; however, this judgement will be more objectively applied where clear guidelines or criteria for the examination are provided. In the absence of guidance and criteria, the examination of candidates becomes dependent on the 'gut feeling' of examiners; effectively, candidates in such a situation 'are being asked to second-guess how an examiner's gut might feel' (Winter *et al.* 2000: 29). There has been a steady improvement in the provision by universities of guidelines and criteria for the award of postgraduate degrees. You should find out as much as you can about the criteria by which your thesis will be judged, so that you can be confident of attaining the examination standard. Universities also provide such guidelines to examiners, so that PhD candidates and examiners can be confident that they are addressing the criteria by which the PhD degree is to be examined.

A questionnaire distributed to thirty-one PhD examiners across a variety of disciplines in the UK revealed considerable consistency in the criteria used by examiners when assessing the PhD thesis. These criteria included:

- conceptual clarity in the design, conduct and analysis of the research;
- intellectual appreciation of the conceptual and theoretical basis of the research, and its limitations and wider significance;
- coherence of argument throughout the thesis;
- appropriate engagement with the literature;
- grasp of methodology;
- presentation of the thesis and compliance with academic conventions;
- originality;
- potential for publication.

(Winter *et al.* 2000: 32–5)

The Institute of Education, University of London, provides its PhD students with relatively detailed guidance on the criteria that are typically used by PhD examiners (see Box 7.1). These criteria should be extremely useful, not least as an excellent basis for discussion with your supervisor on the criteria that are typically used in your university.

Box 7.1 Criteria for assessing a PhD thesis

The following text is reproduced with kind permission of the Institute of Education, University of London.

Criteria for assessing a PhD thesis

Although different examiners will adopt different methods of examining the thesis and for conducting the oral examination, there are some general criteria for evaluating PhD theses which may be useful for students to bear in mind. These are some of the criteria which will be used by examiners when assessing the PhD thesis.

1 Presentation and clarity

- The reader should be able to read the text without difficulty.
- The text should be clear and 'tell a story'.
- The submission should be 'user friendly'. The reader should be able to find his or her way around the submission, locating tables and figures, and being able to cross-reference with ease.

A numbering system for chapters, sections, and, sometimes, paragraphs can be very helpful.

- The style should be economic without unnecessary duplication or repetition.
- The bibliography and/or reference list should be complete and accurate.
- It should be possible to gain easy access to tables and figures relating to particular passages in the text, and to examine both data and commentary without effort.
- The submission should be no longer than necessary. Typically this will mean 75–80,000 words for a PhD, with an absolute maximum of 100,000 words.*

2 Integration and coherence

There should be logical and rational links between the component parts of the thesis. In some cases coherence will be achieved by a series of empirical studies or analyses which build one upon the other. In other words, there will be an intellectual wholeness to the submission.

3 Contribution to knowledge

A submission for a PhD should be approximately equivalent in quantity and quality to at least two articles* of a standard acceptable to a fully refereed journal. Where candidates have already had portions of their doctoral work accepted for publication in such journals, this is *prima facie* evidence of an adequate standard. Alternatively, the submission should be substantial enough to be able to form the basis of a book or research monograph which could meet the standards of an established academic publisher operating a system of critical peer review for book proposals and drafts*.

4 Originality and creativity

The research and the written submission should be the candidate's own work. However, the degree of independence shown may vary according to the research topic, since in some instances students will be working as part of a larger team, while in other instances they will be completely on their own. A candidate should show an appropriate level of independent working.

5 Review of relevant literature

Candidates should demonstrate that they have detailed knowledge of original sources, have a thorough knowledge of the field, and understand the main theoretical and methodological issues. There should not be undue dependence on secondary sources.

The literature review should be more than a catalogue of the literature. It should contain a critical, analytic approach, with an understanding of sources of error and differences of opinion. The literature review should not be over-inclusive. It should not cover non-essential literature nor contain irrelevant digressions. Studies recognised as key or seminal in the field of enquiry should not be ignored. However, a student should not be penalised for omitting to review research published immediately before the thesis was submitted.

A good literature review will be succinct, penetrating and challenging to read.

6 Statement of the research problem

The literature review should have revealed some questions or issues which call for further investigation. Ideally, the problem to be tackled in the research should emerge naturally and inexorably from the literature review.

The research problem may arise as a result of past work which needs to be improved upon. It may be that there is a crucial test which will help to decide between competing theories. The candidate may:

- be proposing a novel theoretical or methodological slant on a topic;
- have created an interesting intellectual friction by bringing together hitherto unrelated fields or topics;
- or have developed a new area of application for a method or theory.

A clear and succinct statement of the research problem should be made, together with a set of specific hypotheses, predictions, or questions which the research is designed to address. There should be some sense that the problem which has been identified is worthwhile.

7 Methods of enquiry adopted

Since determination of the most appropriate methodology is not always a straightforward matter, candidates should justify the methods chosen, with an appropriate rationale in each case.

A project may have a mixture of methodologies, suited to the changing needs of the project as it develops. There may, for instance, be initial semi-structured interviews yielding qualitative data, which can be analysed in a sensitive fashion to yield the building blocks for a more quantitative approach. Or, alternatively, the student may start out with an established quantitative methodology, decide it is inappropriate, and then move to qualitative methods to elicit new questions or issues. There are many variants. Potential alternative methods should be rejected on the basis of a reasoned case.

Candidates should be able to demonstrate that the methods used have been chosen through a conscious process of deliberation; and that the criteria for, and advantages and disadvantages of, particular choices of method are well specified.

There should be a sense of planning. This should include a reasoned consideration of the analytic techniques that the methods chosen will require.

8 Analysis of data

- The analytic methods used need to be justified and need to be shown to be sufficient for the task.
- Any problems arising in the analysis should be recognised and tackled appropriately.
- Candidates should show sensitivity to problems of reliability, measurement error and sources of bias.

- Candidates should understand the assumptions behind the test or tests used.
- Where appropriate, candidates should demonstrate imagination and creativity in identifying and analysing emergent properties of the data which may not have been foreseen.
- The analyses should be clearly linked to the explicit hypotheses, predictions, or questions which formed part of the stated research problem.
- Candidates should be able to demonstrate judgement in the presentation of key summary data within the body of the text, assigning primary data and data of secondary importance to appendices.
- The data should be presented in a well-structured way, so that a clear presentational sequence unfolds.
- In sum, candidates should be able to demonstrate WHY each particular analysis was conducted, HOW the analysis was done, and WHAT the analysis tells us about the data.

9 Discussion of outcomes

- The discussion should summarise, without undue repetition, what has been achieved in the research project.
- It should evaluate the project's contribution to the research area.
- Links should be drawn between the candidate's own work and the work reviewed in the literature review.
- The main findings should be interpreted and related to theory (and practice where appropriate).
- There should be reflection on the research process as a whole. This reveals what the candidate has learned during the course of the work.
- In many cases it will be appropriate to include a section in which the candidate discusses the limitations of the research design and methodology in the light of knowledge acquired whilst undertaking the research, and outlines alternative or additional approaches which might be pursued.
- There should be some pointers to future work, either by the candidate or by others.

- An attempt should be made to identify issues which require further clarification.

* Such detailed requirements vary among universities, and you must check the relevant requirements of your university.

As another example, James Cook University provides a Handbook for Research Higher Degree Students (available at http://www.jcu.edu. au/courses/handbooks/research/), which provides guidelines for PhD students. Appendix G provides guidance on the nature of the PhD, with consideration of the differences that may occur across faculties. Both Appendix I, 'PhD examiner information', and Appendix K, 'Criteria for PhD examiners summary sheet', illustrate the information and guidance on examination criteria for PhD examiners at James Cook University.

Exercise 7.2

1 As a high priority task, find out whether your university provides guidance (similar to that in Box 7.1) on the criteria used by examiners to assess the PhD thesis. Discuss these criteria with your supervisor, with reference to your PhD thesis.

2 If your university does not provide detailed guidance, then discuss with your supervisor the relevance and applicability of criteria in Box 7.1 to the assessment of PhD theses in your university.

The oral examination (viva)

In different countries and institutions there are different conventions and practices that relate to the *viva*. In some countries, there is a public defence at which the examiners, members of academic staff and perhaps members of the public can attend. In other countries, the *viva* is a more private occasion at which only a small number of examiners attend. Here, I focus on the common principles that pertain to the purpose of the *viva*, which combine elements of quality control, assessment and a rite of passage.

Aims of the oral examination (viva)

One of the functions of the rigorous questioning that characterises the PhD *viva* is to establish that the thesis is the student's own work (although the need to establish this is very rare). A more common function of the *viva* is to establish whether the student can explain their understanding of the research background and findings, and justify the methodology that was used. This is particularly important in cases where students have not expressed themselves adequately in the written thesis, and the provisional recommendation is a borderline one. In universities where a *viva* is not normally held, the examiner often has the right to request that a *viva* is conducted so that the candidate can better clarify and explain their research.

Another very common function of the *viva* is to allow a mature and detailed academic discussion between the examiners and the candidate. Such discussion signals the candidate's entry to a community of scholarship and also provides useful feedback that may help improve subsequent publication of the research. This aspect is often under-appreciated by students, who are understandably nervous about the *viva* as an examination that results in a pass or fail result. Nevertheless, despite being nervous beforehand, many students find the *viva* to be an intellectually stimulating and rewarding experience; some students enjoy the *viva*! It is not often that you get an opportunity to have a focused discussion on your research with a small group of experts. Your years of research and intellectual development should mean that you are a world expert in your area of research – whether you realise it or not. The examiners will be genuinely interested in hearing about your new ideas, discussing them, clarifying them and, if necessary, suggesting further improvements.

Preparing for the viva: what kind of questions are asked?

From an analysis of questions that were asked by PhD examiners in twenty-five doctoral *vivas*, Trafford and Leshem (2002) identified predictable, generic questions that investigate the achievement of a doctoral level of research. These questions were identified from a variety of subject disciplines: education, applied sciences, management, bio-medicine, business, history, marketing and psychology. The questions are especially useful because they are conceptual in nature and address the essential characteristics of doctoral research. The generic questions (in bold) are followed by a number of questions that elaborate on the theme of the generic question:

'Why did you choose this topic for your doctoral study?'

'How did you arrive at your conceptual framework?'
- What led you to select these models of . . . ?
- What are the theoretical components of your framework?
- How did you decide upon the variables to include in your conceptual framework?
- How did concepts assist you to visualise and explain what you intended to investigate?
- How did you use your conceptual framework to design your research and analyse your findings?

'How did you arrive at your research design?'
- What other forms of research did you consider?
- How would you explain your research approach?
- Why did you select this particular design for your research?
- What is the link between your conceptual framework and your choice of methodology **and** how would you defend that methodology?
- Can you explain where the data can be found and why your design is the most appropriate way of accessing that data?

'How would you justify your choice of methodology?'
- Please explain your methodology to us.
- Why did you present this in the form of a case study?
- What choices of research approach did you consider as you planned your research?
- Can you tell us about the 'quasi-experimental' research that you used?
- I did not watch your video until after reading your thesis. I wish that I had viewed it earlier – it was very good. Why did you decide to include a video in your thesis? What was its role?

'Why did you decide to use XYZ as your main instrument(s)?'
- How do your methods relate to your conceptual framework?
- Why did you choose to use those methods of data collection?
- What other methods did you consider and why were they rejected?
- How did you handle the data that came from open-ended questions?
- Tell us how you managed to achieve a 100 per cent response

rate from your respondents, who, as adolescents in schools, are not known for complying with such requests!

'How did you select your respondents/materials?'
- How did you decide upon your research boundaries?
- What was the Universe from which your sample was selected and how did you define it?
- What is the relationship between your respondents, the research design and the conceptual framework?
- Why did you choose these respondents rather than other respondents – how do you justify that choice?

'How did you arrive at your conceptual conclusions?'
- What are your conceptual conclusions?
- Were you disappointed with your conclusions?
- How do your conclusions relate to your conceptual framework?
- How did you distinguish between your factual and conceptual conclusions?

'How generalisable are your findings – and why?'
- How did you triangulate your data?
- Were you objective or subjective in your role as a researcher?
- How did you relate the various stages of your research one to another?
- How did you analyse your data, and how did you arrive at meanings from that analysis?

'What is your contribution to knowledge?'
- How important are your findings – and to whom?
- How do your major conclusions link to the work of Rose? (for instance).
- The absence of evidence is not support for what you were investigating, nor is it confirmation of the opposite view. So how do you explain your research outcomes?

'We would like you to criticise your thesis for us.'
- How else might you have undertaken your research?
- What are the strengths and weaknesses of your research?
- What would you do differently if you repeated your research?

'What are YOU going to do after you gain your doctorate?'
- Why did you really want to undertake doctoral study?

- How is gaining your doctorate going to advance your career?
- What are you going to publish from your thesis? (If you have not already thought about this question – please do so now!)

'Is there anything else that you would like to tell us about your thesis which you have not had the opportunity to tell us during the *viva*?'

(Trafford and Leshem 2002: 40–6; kindly provided by the authors, and reproduced with permission from *Higher Education Review* (Tyrell Burgess Associates))

Of course, these precise questions may not be asked in your *viva*; however, very similar questions will aim to assess your understanding of these fundamental issues. Therefore, I strongly recommend that you use these questions to inform your preparation for your *viva*. Consider how to answer these questions in the context of your own work, and think about other variations of these questions that may be more appropriate to your research.

In addition to the 'big issues' identified by the above questions, you can expect other quite specific questions that investigate your depth of knowledge or the thoroughness of your general understanding. Being less predictable, such questions are obviously quite difficult to prepare for, and you will have to trust in your preparation and learning. Nevertheless, your preparation should not overlook some of the more obvious aspects of your research. Some examples from students' *vivas* include the following:

- being asked to discuss some important or controversial papers that were referred to in the thesis;
- being asked to discuss the methodology that was used in an important reference that appeared in the thesis;
- being asked to explain the assumptions and limitations of, for example, an analytical technique or statistical test used in the thesis.

Exercise 7.3

The following checklist prompts you to consider some of the information that you should have in advance of the *viva*.

Do I have a copy of the university documents that stipulate the regulations regarding the conduct of the *viva*?

continued

Have I discussed these regulations with my supervisor?

Have I discussed these regulations and the *viva* with other students (some of whom may have completed their *viva*)?

When are the deadlines for the submission of theses?

Where do I submit the thesis?

How many copies are required?

What accompanying documentation will be required?

Is there an examination fee, and how much is it?

Who will be present at the *viva*?

What are the selection criteria and responsibilities of the internal and external examiners?

Who selects the internal and external examiners?

Is it possible for me to suggest a person who would be an appropriate examiner?

Is it possible for me to indicate a person who is likely to be nominated as an examiner but would be inappropriate (for good reasons)?

Who will inform me of the selection of the examiners, and when?

When the external examiner is made known to me, am I familiar with their research and how their work may complement or conflict with mine?

Am I permitted to view the examiner's report before the *viva*?

Have I discussed my preparation for the *viva* with my supervisor?

Does my supervisor agree with my identification of the original contribution to knowledge of my thesis?

Am I satisfied that I can answer questions similar to those identified by Trafford and Leshem (2002, see above)?

Where will the *viva* take place (building and room number)?

Will I be expected to make a presentation; if not, can I request to give one?

At what time will the *viva* take place?

Where should I wait before the *viva*?

Who will be chairman at the *viva*?

Will there be a short break after one hour (for example)?

After the *viva*, will I be expected to attend a reception/meal with the examiners?

You may receive further information from your supervisor, other students and students who have recently completed the *viva*.

General advice for the *viva*

The external examiner may (more usually) or may not chair the oral exam, and usually asks the majority of the questions. The external examiner is typically a recognised expert in a research discipline relevant to the thesis. Also in attendance is an internal examiner, who will also ask questions. Your supervisor may or may not be present. The details of practice vary among universities, and you will almost certainly be well informed about the particular practices that occur in your department. If not, ask well in advance to be sure that you are aware of what will happen. No two *vivas* are the same; nevertheless, while the following general comments may not apply in every *viva*, they are indicative of typical patterns.

You should know who the external examiner will be, well before the *viva*. You may have communicated with the person during your research, and may have met them at a conference or meeting. In such cases, you are likely to be reasonably familiar with the external examiner's background. If not, become familiar with their research interests, read their main publications, and identify common interests (or disagreements) between their work and yours.

In terms of duration, most *vivas* last between one and three hours. The atmosphere in a PhD *viva* is usually professional, but courteous to the point of being friendly. Some examiners may be more formal than others, but most will want to put you at ease; this is where some knowledge about the examination style of the examiner will be particularly helpful. Unfortunately, there are horror stories of exceptionally confrontational examiners; on the whole, these are uncommon. On the other hand, don't let your guard down because the examiners are very pleasant and friendly. The examiners have an important job to do, and academics can be adept at veiling their strong questioning or criticism.

Above all else, be prepared. Read the generic questions identified by Trafford and Leshem (2002, reproduced above) and consider how you would answer these and similar questions as they apply to your research. Ask your supervisor for help in preparing for the *viva*.

On the day of the *viva*, bring a copy of your thesis, a pen and blank paper with you. You may be asked to refer to certain sections of the thesis (if so, you should be given time to read these sections). The pages of your copy of the thesis should be numbered the same as the examiners' copies, which will aid reference. It may be helpful to have labelled 'Post-it' notes indicating the beginning of chapters or sections that you consider are particularly important or likely to be referred to.

In many countries, it is traditional for the student to make a presentation (which is sometimes quite lengthy) of their research findings. In countries where this has not been traditional practice, it is becoming more common for a short presentation to be made at the *viva*. Making an oral presentation temporarily puts you in control, and is an opportunity for you to impress (as one example of relevant advice, see Booth 1993); however, ensure that you are well prepared, have practised the presentation beforehand and are familiar with the available facilities. For those making an electronic presentation, it would be prudent to have an overhead projector and transparencies on standby, just in case.

The *viva* proper is characterised by the external and internal examiners asking you questions. Listen carefully to the questions. Consider any question for a few moments before answering – don't blurt out the first thing that comes into your head. Do not answer simply 'yes' or 'no' to questions; on the other hand, do not give a prepared speech. Try to answer the question as it is put, remembering that you are engaged in an academic conversation. If you are unsure of the answer to a difficult or speculative question, then be prepared to admit that you are uncertain, but could speculate on the answer. If you don't understand the question, ask the examiner to repeat the question, or repeat your interpretation to the examiner. If you still don't understand the question, or understand but can't answer it, then it is better to admit it than to try and bluff.

It is very important that you are prepared to justify your ideas and conclusions. If the examiners challenge your interpretation but you feel that your case is a good one, muster your arguments and be willing to present your case firmly but courteously. Stay calm and pleasant, and present your points based on the evidence; do not be emotive or defensive. However, if the examiners have identified a genuine weakness, accept their advice and indicate that this will be addressed. Even if you feel the examiners are unreasonably critical, do not become argumentative or allow the discussion to become heated. You can agree to differ and to reconsider the point.

Do not be overly worried that some parts of the exam were very difficult – it is only by pushing you to your limits that the examiners can determine your ability.

After the examination

Examination results

The detailed grades of the PhD examination vary among universities, and it is important that you discover all available information and regulations that pertain to your particular university. However, the PhD grades are likely to reflect the following range:

1   *Award of degree without any revision.* This is relatively rare.
2   *Award of degree subject to minor revision.* This is the most common result, and typically only requires minor typographical corrections, or minimal editorial changes.
3   *Award of degree subject to substantial revision (without re-examination).* Such a decision usually requires a modest amount of work to rectify limited deficiencies, e.g. the clarification of several paragraphs or sections, improved presentation, minor changes to some figures or tables, or some data analysis. The examiners may require the supervisor or Head of Department to ensure that the revision is completed. In some cases, the examiners may inspect the thesis (without re-examination) to ensure that the revision is completed to their satisfaction.
4   *Major revision required and resubmit thesis with re-examination (a.k.a. a referral).* This result may occur when a thesis has been submitted prematurely, and requires further research to be conducted and reported, or an improved presentation of the existing research. The latter requirement may involve rewriting, re-analysis and reinterpretation to an extent that may affect the main conclusions of the thesis. Once the major revision requested by the examiners has been completed, it would be expected that the thesis would attain the expected standard for award of the PhD degree.
5   *Award of MPhil.* The award of MPhil (a lower degree) may occur in cases where the examiners believe that the thesis will not be improved sufficiently to attain the standard of PhD, but still contains some research of merit. This may be because the submitted thesis is lacking in originality or does not make a significant contribution to knowledge. Some revision may be required before award of MPhil.
6   *Fail.* This is an extremely rare result and would apply to research so seriously flawed that it is irredeemable.

At the end of the oral examination, PhD candidates are requested to leave while the examiners discuss their recommended result. The candidate is then invited back in and informed of the recommended result.

At this stage, most candidates are required to undertake either minor or major revisions. It is important that you receive a written list of the requested revisions, which reduces any potential misunderstanding about what is expected to attain the required standard. There will be a deadline by which you will have to complete the revisions, or resubmit the thesis.

Appeals

Here, I simply wish to make you aware that university regulations provide details of procedures that are available to students to submit an appeal against a decision not to award a degree, or not to allow resubmission for a degree. Some typical examples of where an appeal might arise include: irregularities in the examination procedures; exceptional circumstances that affected your performance, of which the examiners were not aware when making their decision; and evidence of prejudice, bias or inadequate assessment by one of the examiners. Such appeals must usually be made in writing within a specified duration after the examination, and must state clearly the evidence on which the appeal is based.

Exercise 7.4

1   You should find out the following information in advance of the *viva*:

(a) Who will inform me of the examiners' decision, and when?

(b) Who will inform me of any revisions that need to be made?

(c) Will these revisions be provided in a written format so that I am fully aware of the issues that need to be addressed to bring the thesis up to the required standard?

(d) How soon after the *viva* is the deadline for submission of the final version, with any corrections?

(e) When is the next graduation ceremony?

2 After the *viva*:

    (a) How much time is permitted before the thesis is to be resubmitted?

    (b) If dissatisfied with the conduct of the examination, am I aware of the appeals procedures that relate to the PhD examination? How soon after the examination must an appeal be lodged?

Professional development for your career

A number of references in the 'Recommended reading' list discuss the career prospects of PhD students and the transition from being a PhD student to the next stage of your career. Your university may also provide information and resources to assist with career planning.

After you receive the PhD degree and are seeking employment, it is worth returning to the list of transferable skills in Chapter 1 (Box 1.3) to remind yourself how the doctoral project can contribute to your employability. Related to the identification of transferable skills, Doncaster and Thorne (2000) describe the professional doctorate (DProf), which tends to consist of a structured programme of study, part of which is taught and part of which is based on a dissertation. It is aimed at the professional needs of practitioners to engage in continuing professional development – 'scholarly professionals' – rather than 'professional scholars' for whom the traditional PhD tends to be an initiation into an academic research career. They identified a number of high-level capabilities that describe a variety of high-level skills that DProf candidates had to implement in the course of their professional career and describe in their dissertation. As many PhD students pursue careers as 'scholarly professionals' (rather than continuing as 'professional scholars'), these generic high-level capabilities provide a useful indication of the standard of performance that a doctoral graduate may aim for in (or expect from) a professional work environment. These capabilities include:

1 High-level transferable skills
    Habitual reflection on own and others professional practice
    Awareness of political implications of doctoral work
    Self-directed and self-managed learning

Ability to tackle unpredictable problems in novel ways
Ability to engage in full professional and academic communication with others in their field
Ability to evaluate, select, combine and use a range of research methods
Contribute to the development of applied research methodology.

2 High-level cognitive abilities
Interdisciplinary knowledge
The ability to work at current limits of theoretical and/or research understanding in particular fields
The ability to deal with complexity and contradictions in the knowledge base
The ability to synthesise ideas and create responses to problems that redefine or extend existing knowledge
The ability to evaluate alternative approaches.

3 Operational context
Ability to function in complex, unpredictable and specialised work contexts which require innovative study
Autonomy within bounds of professional practice with high levels of responsibility for self and others
Awareness of ethical dilemmas likely to arise in research and professional practice
The ability to formulate solutions in dialogue with stakeholders.

4 Capacity to bring about organisational change within one's professional practice
Identifying where there is a need for change
Designing interventions to bring about specified changes
Implementing the interventions
Evaluating the interventions for their impact on the targeted work situation
Identifying further needs for change, etc.

(Doncaster and Thorne 2000: 393–4)

Thus, while the award of DProf requires candidates to demonstrate their implementation of these capabilities, I suggest that the PhD graduate may expect to implement such capabilities in their future professional career. Obviously, there are some limitations to the suggestion that these capabilities automatically translate into high-level transferable skills for

PhD graduates. Nevertheless, most of these generic capabilities are a useful representation of the challenges and expectations that may face PhD graduates. At the least, these high-level skills should encourage you to think about how your PhD training contributes to your career development and helps prepare you for your future profession.

Recommended reading

Publications

Cryer, P. (2000) *The Research Student's Guide to Success*, Buckingham: Open University Press.
See Chapters 20 and 21 'Producing your thesis'; 'Preparing for and conducting yourself in the examination'. See also Chapter 22 'Afterwards!'

Murray, R. (2003) *How to Survive Your Viva: Defending a Thesis in an Oral Examination*, Maidenhead: Open University Press.

Tinkler, P. and Jackson, C. (2004) *The Doctoral Examination Process: A Handbook for Students, Examiners, and Supervisors*, Maidenhead: Society for Research into Higher Education/Open University Press.

Online resources

'What goalposts?' by John Wakeford.
   http://education.guardian.co.uk/higher/postgraduate/story/0,12848,890233, 00.html
PhD students' (negative) experience of PhD examination.

'After the PhD, what's next?' by Carol Ng.
http://nextwave.sciencemag.org/cgi/content/full/2002/10/31/2

'Starting out' (on a career in research) and 'Getting on' by Kirstie Urquhart and 'On the horns of a dilemma' by Sowmya Viswanathan (and the related articles) discuss the pursuit of a career in academia:
http://nextwave.sciencemag.org/cgi/content/full/2003/09/24/4
http://nextwave.sciencemag.org/cgi/content/full/2003/10/08/1
http://nextwave.sciencemag.org/cgi/content/full/2003/01/02/2

'Landing an academic job: the process and the pitfalls' by Jon Dantzig.
http://quattro.me.uiuc.edu/~jon/ACAJOB/Latex2e/academic_job.pdf

Appendix 1

Originality

The following list provides different interpretations of originality in the context of doctoral research (modified from Phillips and Pugh 1994: 61–2):

1 Setting down a major piece of new information in writing for the first time.
2 Continuing a previously original piece of work.
3 Carrying out original work designed by the supervisor.
4 Providing a single original technique, observation or result in an otherwise unoriginal but competent piece of research.
5 Having many original ideas, methods and interpretation all performed by others but under the direction of the research student.
6 Showing originality in testing someone else's idea.
7 Carrying out empirical work that has not been done before.
8 Making a synthesis that has not been done before.
9 Using already known material but with a new interpretation.
10 Trying out something in your own country that has previously only been done in other countries.
11 Taking a particular technique and applying it in a new area.
12 Bringing new evidence to bear on an old issue.
13 Being cross-disciplinary and using different methodologies.
14 Looking at areas that people in the discipline have not looked at before.
15 Adding to knowledge in a way that has not previously been done before.

A list of about twenty interpretations of originality is also provided in Winter et al. (2000), based on a survey of the criteria that PhD examiners use. Generally, there is considerable overlap with the list by Phillips and

Pugh (1994). Some examples of originality from Winter *et al.*'s study are as follows:

- Makes an original contribution to knowledge or understanding of the subject, in topic area, in method, in experimental design, in theoretical synthesis, or engagement with conceptual issues.
- Contains innovation, speculation, imaginative reconstruction, cognitive excitement: 'the author has clearly wrestled with the method, trying to shape it to gain new insights'.
- Is comprehensive in its theoretical linkages or makes novel connections between areas of knowledge.
- Is innovative in content and adventurous in method, obviously at the leading edge in its particular field, with potential for yielding new knowledge.
- Applies established techniques to novel patterns, or devises new techniques which allow new questions to be addressed.

(Winter *et al.* 2000: 35)

Appendix 2

Answers to exercises

Exercise 3.4

Publication practices

Hypothetical scenarios raise many different issues that can be discussed and debated. The observations and questions given below suggest just some of the areas that can be explored.

Contributions to a scientific field are not counted in terms of the number of papers. They are counted in terms of significant differences in how science is understood. With that in mind, Paula and her students need to consider how they are most likely to make a significant contribution to their field. One determinant of impact is the coherence and completeness of a paper. Paula and her students may need to begin writing before they can tell whether one or more papers is needed.

In retrospect, Paula and her students might also ask themselves about the process that led to their decision. Should they have discussed publications much earlier in the process? Were the students led to believe that they would be first authors on published papers? If so, should that influence future work in the lab?

(reproduced from NAS 1995)

Exercise 5.3

Adams, D. (2001)
Andrews, D. (2000)
Baker, J. (1999)
Baker, J. and Adams, S. (1998)
Baker, J., Adams, S. and Barrett, T. (1997)

Frank, A. (1987)
Frank, G. (1985)
Frank, A. and McCann, M. (1980)
Gavin, B. (2000)

Exercise 5.4

Brent, E.E. 1986. The computer-assisted literature review. *Computers and the Social Sciences* **2**: 137–151.

Dewhurst, D.G., Macleod, H.A. and Norris, T.A.M. 2000. Independent student learning aided by computers: an acceptable alternative to lectures? *Computers and Education* **35**: 223–241.

Eklundh, K.S. 1994. Linear and non-linear strategies in computer-based writing. *Computers and Composition* **11**: 203–216.

Heinich, R., Molenda, M., Russell, J.D. and Smaldino, S.E. 1996. *Instructional Media and Technologies for Learning*. Englewood Cliffs: Prentice-Hall.

McGowan, C. and Sendall, P. 1997. Using the World Wide Web to enhance writing assignments in introductory chemistry courses. *Journal of Chemistry and Education* **74**: 391–392.

Marshall, S. 2001. Reference management software: it's your choice. *Technical Computing* **22**: 16.

Szabo, A. and Hastings, N. 2000. Using IT in the undergraduate classroom: should we replace the blackboard with PowerPoint? *Computers and Education* **35**: 175–187.

Note also the change in the sequence of the references to ensure that they are in alphabetical order.

For further exercises, see:
http://www.ucc.ie/research/stars/referencing.html

References

Alton-Lee, A. (1998) 'A troubleshooter's checklist for prospective authors derived from reviewers' critical feedback', *Teaching and Teacher Education*, 14: 887–90.

Austin, R. (2002) 'Project management and discovery', *Next Wave*, 13 September. Online. Available HTTP: <http://nextwave.sciencemag.org/cgi/content/full/2002/09/10/4>(accessed 7 July 2004).

Baker, S. and Baker, K. (2000) *The Complete Idiot's Guide® to Project Management*, 2nd edn, Indianapolis: Alpha Books.

Barass, R. (2002) *Scientists Must Write: A Guide to Better Writing for Scientists, Engineers and Students*, 2nd edn, London: Routledge.

Bem, D.J. (1995) 'Writing a review article for psychological bulletin', *Psychological Bulletin*, 118: 172–7. Online. Available HTTP: <http://comp9.psych.cornell.edu/dbem/psych_bull.html> (accessed 6 June 2004).

Berry, R. (1986) *How to Write a Research Paper*, Oxford: Pergamon.

Booth, V. (1993) *Communicating in Science: Writing a Scientific Paper and Speaking at Scientific Meetings*, 2nd edn, Cambridge: Cambridge University Press.

Brown, G. and Atkins, M. (1988) *Effective Teaching in Higher Education*, London: Routledge.

Bruce, C.S. (1994) 'Research students' early experiences of the dissertation literature review', *Studies in Higher Education*, 19: 217–29.

Caffarella, R.S. and Barnett, B.G. (2000) 'Teaching doctoral students to become scholarly writers: the importance of giving and receiving critiques', *Studies in Higher Education*, 25: 39–51.

Cambridge, B. (1994) 'Revision works! A conversation between an author and JTW editors', *Journal of Teaching Writing*, 13: 7–13.

Cassey, P. and Blackburn, T.M. (2003) 'Publication rejection among ecologists', *Trends in Ecology and Evolution*, 18: 375–6.

Clough, P. and Nutbrown, C. (2002) *A Student's Guide to Methodology*, London: Sage.

Cohen, J.E. (1995) *How Many People Can the Earth Support?*, New York: W.W. Norton.

Cryer, P. (2000) *The Research Student's Guide to Success*, Buckingham: Open University Press.

Doncaster, K. and Thorne, L. (2000) 'Reflection and planning: essential elements of professional doctorates', *Reflective Practice*, 1: 391–9.

Elbow, P. (1998) *Writing Without Teachers*, 2nd edn, Oxford: Oxford University Press.

Finn, J.A. and Crook, A.C. (2003) 'Research skills training for undergraduate researchers: the pedagogical approach of the STARS project', *Bioscience Education Electronic journal*, vol. 2, article 1. Online journal. Available HTTP: <http://bio.ltsn.ac.uk/journal> (accessed 6 July 2004).

Flanagin, A., Carey, L.A., Fontanarosa, P.B., Phillips, S.G., Pace, B.P., Lundberg, G.D. and Rennie, D. (1998) 'Prevalence of articles with honorary authors and ghost authors in peer-reviewed medical journals', *The Journal of the American Medical Association*, 280: 222–4. Online. Available HTTP: <http://www.ama-assn.org/public/peer/7_15_98/jpv80004.htm> (accessed 6 July 2004).

Francis, H. (1997) 'The research process', in N. Graves and V. Varma (eds) *Working for a Doctorate: A Guide for the Humanities and Social Sciences*, London: Routledge.

Golde, C.M. (2001) *Survey on Doctoral Education and Career Preparation*. Online. Available HTTP: <http://www.phd-survey.org/advice/advice.htm> (accessed 6 July 2004).

Guilford, C. (1996) 'Paradigm online writing assistant'. Online. Available HTTP: <http://www.powa.org> (accessed 8 July 2004).

Hammer, V.N. (1992) 'Misconduct in science: do scientists need a professional code of ethics?' Online. Available HTTP: <http://www.chem.vt.edu/chem-ed/ethics/vinny/www_ethx.html> (accessed 6 July 2004).

Hartley, J. (1994a) *Designing Instructional Text*, London: Kogan Page.

Hartley, J. (1994b) 'Three ways to improve the clarity of journal abstracts', *British Journal of Educational Psychology*, 64: 331–43.

Hartley, J. (1997) 'Writing the thesis', in N. Graves and V. Varma (eds) *Working for a Doctorate: A Guide for the Humanities and Social Sciences*, London: Routledge.

Hartley, J. (2000) 'Clarifying the abstracts of systematic literature reviews', *Bulletin of the Medical Library Association*, 88: 332–7. Online. Available HTTP: <http://www.pubmedcentral.nih.gov/articlerender.fcgi?artid=35254> (accessed 6 July 2004).

Hartley, J.R. and Branthwaite, A. (1989) 'The psychologist as wordsmith: a questionnaire study of the writing strategies of productive British psychologists', *Higher Education*, 18: 423–52.

Hockey, J. (1997) 'A complex craft: United Kingdom PhD supervision in the social sciences', *Research in Post-Compulsory Education*, 2: 45–70.

Houston, R.A. (2002). 'Madness and gender in the long eighteenth century', *Social History*, 27: 309–26.

Jackson, P. and Tinkler, C. (2001) 'Back to basics: a consideration of the purposes of the PhD *viva*', *Assessment and Evaluation in Higher Education*, 26: 355–66.

Johnston, S. (1997) 'Examining the examiners: an analysis of examiners' reports on doctoral theses', *Studies in Higher Education*, 22: 333–47.

Keay, J. (2000) *The Great Arc: The Dramatic Tale of How India was Mapped and Everest was Named*, London: HarperCollins.

Kepner, C.H. and Tregoe, B.B. (1997) *The New Rational Manager*, 2nd edn, Princeton, NJ: Princeton Research Press.

Kerzner, H. (2003) *Project Management: A Systems Approach to Planning, Scheduling, and Controlling*, 8th edn, New York: Wiley.

Kleijn, D. and Sutherland, W.J. (2003) 'How effective are European agri-environment schemes in conserving and promoting biodiversity?', *Journal of Applied Ecology*, 40: 947–69.

Lawton, D. (1997) 'How to succeed in postgraduate study', in N. Graves and V. Varma (eds) *Working for a Doctorate: A Guide for the Humanities and Social Sciences*, London: Routledge.

Lindsay, D. (1995) *A Guide to Scientific Writing*, 2nd edn, Melbourne: Longman Cheshire.

Lock, D. (1988) *Project Management*, 4th edn, Aldershot: Gower.

Menuhin, Y. (1972) *Theme and Variations*, New York: Stein and Day.

Mullins, G. and Kiley, M. (2002) '"It's a PhD, not a Nobel Prize": how experienced examiners assess research theses', *Studies in Higher Education*, 27: 369–86.

Murray, R. (2002) *How to Write a Thesis*, Maidenhead: Open University Press.

Murray, R. and Lowe, A. (1995) 'Writing and dialogue for the PhD', *Journal of Graduate Education*, 1: 103–9.

National Academy of Sciences (1995) *On Being a Scientist: Responsible Conduct in Research*, Washington: National Academic Press. Online. Available HTTP: <http://stills.nap.edu/readingroom/books/obas/> (accessed 6 July 2004).

National Postgraduate Committee (1992) *Guidelines for Codes of Practice for Postgraduate Research*. Online. Available HTTP: <http://www.npc.org.uk/page/1003801720> (accessed 6 July 2004).

National Postgraduate Committee (1995) *Guidelines on Accommodation and Facilities for Postgraduate Research*. Online. Available HTTP: <http://www.npc.org.uk/page/1003802081> (accessed 6 July 2004).

Northedge, A., Thomas, J., Lane, A. and Peasgood, A. (1997) *The Sciences Good Study Guide*, Milton Keynes: Open University Press.

Peat, J., Elliot, E., Baur, L. and Keena, V. (2002) *Scientific Writing: Easy When You Know How*, London: BMJ Books.

Phillips, E.M. and Pugh, D.S. (1994) *How to Get a PhD: A Handbook for Students and their Supervisors*, 2nd edn, Buckingham: Open University Press.

Plevin, R. (1996) 'Be sweet, supervisor', *New Scientist*, 3 August, p. 46.

Pole, C. (2000) 'Technicians and scholars in pursuit of the PhD: some reflections on doctoral study', *Research Papers in Education*, 15: 95–111.

Portny, S. (2002) 'Project management in an uncertain environment', *Next Wave*, 23 August. Online. Available HTTP: <http://nextwave.sciencemag.org/cgi/content/full/2002/08/21/3> (accessed 7 July 2004).

Potter, S. (ed.) (2002) *Doing Postgraduate Research*, London: Sage.

Pratt, J.M. (1984) 'Writing your thesis', *Chemistry in Britain*, December: 1114–15.

Shaw, D. and Abouzeid, S. (2002) 'Navigating through the maze: the practical issues of conducting research for novices', *Journal of Graduate Education*, 3: 54–64.

Strunk, W. (1918) *Elements of Style*, Ithaca, NY: Private print. [Geneva, NY: Press of W.P. Humphrey]; Bartleby.com, 1999. Online. Available HTTP: <http://www.bartleby.com/141/> (accessed 6 July 2004).

Tinkler, P. and Jackson, C. (2000) 'Examining the doctorate: institutional policy and the PhD examination process in Britain', *Studies in Higher Education*, 25: 167–80.

Trafford, V. and Leshem, S. (2002) 'Starting at the end to undertake doctoral research: predictable questions as stepping stones', *Higher Education Review*, 35: 31–49.

The University of Reading (2004) *Code of Practice on Research Students*. Online. Available HTTP: <http://www.rdg.ac.uk/Handbooks/Teaching_and_Learning/Code_of_Practice.doc> (accessed 6 July 2004).

Verma, G.K. and Beard, R.M. (1981) *What is Educational Research?: Perspectives on Techniques of Research*, Aldershot: Gower.

Veroff, J. (2001) 'Writing', in K.E. Rudestam and R.R. Newton (eds) *Surviving Your Dissertation: A Comprehensive Guide to Content and Process*, Thousand Oaks, CA: Sage.

White, M. and Gribbin, J. (1994) *Einstein: A Life in Science*, London: Pocket Books.

Wield, D. (2002) 'Planning and organising a research project', in S. Potter (ed.) *Doing Postgraduate Research*, London: Sage.

Winter, R., Griffiths, M. and Green, K. (2000) 'The academic qualities of practice: what are the criteria for a practice-based PhD?', *Studies in Higher Education*, 25: 25–37.

Index